ASIAN FRONTIERS

Other works by ALASTAIR LAMB

Britain and Chinese Central Asia: The Road to Lhasa, 1767–1905, London 1960

Chandi Bukit Batu Pahat: The Excavation and Reconstruction of an Ancient Temple in Kedah, Singapore 1960

British Missions to Cochin China, 1778–1822, Singapore 1961

Miscellaneous Papers on Early Hindu and Buddhist Settlement in Northern Malaya and Southern Thailand, Kuala Lumpur 1961

The China-India Border: The Origins of the Disputed Boundaries, London 1964

The McMahon Line: A Study in the Relations Between India, China and Tibet, 1904 to 1914: Vol. I: Morley, Minto and Non-Interference in Tibet, Vol. II: Hardinge, McMahon and the Simla Conference; London 1966

Crisis in Kashmir, 1947 to 1966, London 1966

Alastair Lamb

ASIAN FRONTIERS
Studies in a Continuing Problem

PALL MALL PRESS
LONDON

Published by the Pall Mall Press Ltd
77–79 Charlotte Street, London W1

© Australian Institute of International Affairs

FIRST PUBLISHED 1968

SBN 269. 99298. 7

Printed in Great Britain by
The Camelot Press Ltd, London and Southampton

To
SABINA LAMB
As a small token of gratitude for
all she has done for me

Contents

Maps

Acknowledgements

This book emerged from a series of seminars which I gave at the Australian National University in 1965; and I would like to thank Sir Keith Hancock and my colleagues at Canberra who were my audience and whose comments were so stimulating. The bulk of the book was written in Leeds; and the work was made possible by the Leverhulme Trust and by Professors Borras and Lattimore of the University of Leeds. Dr Lo Hui-min of the Australian National University and Professor J. A. S. Grenville of the University of Leeds most kindly read early drafts of the typescript: I am most grateful for their observations and criticisms. The maps I drew myself, with much useful advice from my wife and from my father-in-law, Ashley Havinden, whose great experience in the technicalities of line drawing for reproduction was most valuable to me; but I must take full responsibility for such defects in these maps as might offend the eye of the professional cartographer. Finally, I would like to express my appreciation for the patient care with which Derick Mirfin helped me see this book through the press.

Leeds, November 1967   A. L.

Introductory:
The Problem and the Scene

With the defeat of Germany in 1945, the Soviet Union emerged as by far the most powerful state on the Eurasian continent. It can be argued with some conviction that, as much as anything else, the 'cold war' of the late 1940s and early 1950s was concerned with the definition of the western limits of the Soviet empire. To the West, that is to say to the United States and its allies, the main objective in such conflicts as the civil war in Greece in 1947 and the Berlin crisis of 1948 was to prevent Soviet influence from spreading beyond the frontiers established during the concluding stages of the Second World War. This intention was usually expressed in ideological terms: the containment of communism; but it could equally well be defined in a language of international politics which would not have seemed strange to the diplomatists assembled at the Congress of Vienna in 1815.

By 1960, the West—and probably the Soviet Union as well—had achieved the main political goal of the 'cold war'. A stable line of demarcation (what Winston Churchill first dubbed the 'iron curtain'), separated the Soviet sphere from that of the Western alliance dominated by the power of the United States of America. Stability was achieved in a number of ways: by Western intervention in civil war in Greece in 1947 and by

Western non-intervention in anti-Russian rebellion in Hungary in 1956; by confrontation short of war, as in Berlin in 1948; by physical measures of frontier control, like the Berlin wall built in 1961; by agreement between the two sides to treat certain areas as neutral zones, as in the case of Austria in 1955. Once the major line of demarcation had been settled, the political evolution of the nation-states of Europe could take place in a far less restrictive atmosphere than would otherwise have been possible. The loosening of the Soviet grip on Eastern Europe and the decline in the effectiveness of NATO are both direct consequences of the conversion of the 'iron curtain' from an uneasy cease-fire line into an integral part of the accepted frontier system of Europe.

In Asia, unlike Europe, the process of major frontier demarcation still continues. Conflicts like the Vietnam war, there can be no doubt, have for the major parties involved a significance very similar to that detected at an earlier period in the civil conflict in Greece. Just as the Western victory in Greece was a crucial stage in the definition of the post-war limits of Soviet influence in the Balkans, so the outcome in Vietnam will produce a definition of the limits of Western influence in mainland South-east Asia. In two important respects, however, the present situation in Asia is far more complex than was the situation obtaining in Europe in the late 1940s. In the first place, great power diplomacy in Asia has become inextricably involved with the aftermath of colonialism and the complicated evolution of local nationalist aspirations. Vietnam, for example, provides a multitude of instances of the conflicts between indigenous and external political aims—conflicts extremely difficult to resolve without the reimposition of some form of colonial government. In the second place, where in Europe there were in effect but two major protagonists, the United States and the Soviet Union, in Asia there are now three with the emergence of communist China as a great power. The Chinese factor would be of lesser significance were there still remaining a basic identity of

Sino-Russian policy; but since the late 1950s such identity has well nigh disappeared.

The present crisis in Asia is taking place on two distinct, though interconnected, levels. There is the superstructure of great power competition, more complex than in Europe because it is essentially tripartite rather than bipartite. There is a sub-stratum of indigenous Asian politics involving in many cases the surge of national and regional forces which were masked or suppressed until very recently by colonial rule. At both levels, the crisis can be interpreted in terms of frontier policy; that is to say, in terms of drawing lines on maps and establishing on the actual ground lines so drawn. The Sino-Soviet, Sino-American and Soviet-American struggles will, if and when they are resolved, produce definitions of spheres of influence or interest capable of geographical expression, just as one can now define cartographically where the stabilised 'iron curtain' runs across Europe. The creation of such Asian 'curtains' will make it possible to create or maintain under their shelter systems of subsidiary frontiers. Will there be two Vietnams or one? Where will the final Indo-Pakistani border run in Kashmir? Questions such as these can be answered only when the major geopolitical divides have been settled; yet the task of defining the major frontiers is enormously complicated by tensions arising from subsidiary boundary problems, the settlement of which was deferred or distorted by the period of colonial rule on the Asian continent.

The history and politics of frontiers have long tended to be neglected subjects, as Lord Curzon pointed out in his 1907 Romanes Lecture in the University of Oxford. On the basis of his great knowledge of Asian affairs acquired through travel, research and practical experience as viceroy of India, Curzon observed that

Frontiers are the chief anxiety of nearly every Foreign Office in the civilised world, and are the subject of four out of every

five political treaties or conventions that are concluded. . . .
Frontier policy is of the first practical importance, and has a
more profound effect upon the peace or warfare of nations
than any other factor, political or economic.

Yet, he continued, the literature on frontier questions would
barely fill a single library shelf. It cannot be said that the study
of frontier policy has flourished markedly since 1907; and in this
fact lies the main arguable justification for the present book,
which seeks to examine the modern international history of
Asia in terms of frontiers and boundaries. It is not claimed that
frontiers and boundaries are the only factors involved, merely
that they are important factors deserving of more serious study
than is generally accorded to them. Frontiers, after all, lie close
to the heart of foreign policy for they involve both the identity
and the security of the sovereign state in which political, social,
economic and ideological processes take place.

★

A useful distinction has sometimes been made between the terms
'boundary' and 'frontier'. A boundary is a clear divide between
sovereignties which can be marked as a line on a map. It has, as
it were, length but not area. The Curzon Line between Russia
and Poland, and the Oder-Neisse Line of recent German history;
the Durand Line between what is now Pakistan and Afghanistan, and the McMahon Line between India and Tibet; the 17th
parallel in Vietnam, the 38th parallel in Korea, and the 49th
parallel separating Canada from the United States of America—
these are all examples of a boundary in this sense. If the boundary is capable of being set out on the map, and if it is explicitly
accepted by the states which it divides even though they have
not got down to the task of setting up boundary posts or otherwise laying down the boundary on the ground—a situation
which frequently arises where the boundary passes through
difficult country—then that boundary is said to have been

delimited. If the boundary has also been marked out on the ground, then it is said to have been *demarcated*. A properly demarcated boundary should be free from disputes if the parties concerned accept the validity of the act of demarcation. A delimited boundary may well produce disputes arising from differing interpretations of its verbal or cartographic definition. The boundary between Thailand and Cambodia, for example, was delimited by treaty in 1904; and both states, though perhaps with a measure of reluctance, accept the validity of the treaty. Yet there has been a most acrimonious argument between them as to the exact whereabouts of the treaty boundary on the ground. On which side of the line should the Preah Vihear temple be? The settlement of this dispute by the International Court of Justice in 1962 was intended to produce a demarcation of the boundary in the Preah Vihear region at least, though the Thais have not, it would seem, entirely reconciled themselves to this decision. (See page 169 below.)

Many stretches of boundary in Asia have neither been delimited nor demarcated. Much of the Sino-Indian border falls into this category, as does also the extreme western end of the boundary between Chinese Sinkiang and the Soviet Union. In some cases such boundaries follow natural features so clear and so suitable for boundary-making that they have been accepted *de facto*. No urgent need has been felt for the processes of delimitation and demarcation. In other cases, such boundaries are, in effect, no more than arbitrary lines drawn by cartographers on maps of unpopulated and difficult country—perhaps inadequately surveyed—in which the process of boundary evolution has not yet reached a stage where delimitation and demarcation would be called for. Much of the border between British India and Sinkiang and Tibet was still of this kind when the British left the subcontinent in 1947. Here, in British times, a situation calling for delimitation or demarcation did not arise. It has, of course, arisen now with the development of the Sino-Indian boundary dispute; and an inevitable consequence of the

settlement of that dispute will be the delimitation and demarca-
'ion of the boundary.*

Much of the terrain through which the Sino-Indian border
runs does not, in fact, provide the kind of natural features
which facilitate boundary settlement. There is a natural *zone*
for the boundary, somewhere along the Himalayan range,
which is not in serious doubt; there is not, however, a particularly obvious natural *line*, despite much Indian argument
about the sanctity of watersheds. Within the Himalayas there
exist many watersheds, and the great problem is to decide
which particular watershed should be the Sino-Indian border.
We shall return to this question later on. The point of immediate
significance is that much of the Sino-Indian border along the
Himalayas represents a *frontier* rather than a *boundary*.

A frontier, as that term was understood by authorities on
British imperial border questions, such as Lord Curzon and Sir
Henry McMahon, is a *zone* rather than a *line*. It is a tract of
territory separating the centres of two sovereignties. An
example would be the region generally known as the North-
West Frontier: the zone lying between the British-administered
territory of the Indus plains and the sphere of authority of the
Afghan government. A frontier zone may well be of very extensive area, and a dispute over the exact whereabouts of a boundary line through a frontier zone can involve large tracts of
territory. The Sino-Indian boundary dispute, because it concerns such a line through a frontier zone, involves more than
50,000 square miles of territory. Thus, boundary disputes can
also be territorial disputes as well.

Boundaries and frontiers can be most usefully studied,
perhaps, in the context of their function or purpose. There are
important differences, for example, between the boundary of a

* The boundary between China and Pakistan was delimited in the
Sino-Pakistani boundary agreement of March 1963. It has subsequently
been demarcated on the ground by a joint Sino-Pakistani boundary
commission. India has refused to accept the validity of these proceedings.

sovereign nation-state and that of a colonial possession. The change in status from colony to fully independent state may have the most profound boundary consequences. Let us consider here in rather general terms some of the main categories of boundary and frontier.

The boundary of the fully independent nation-state is the cell wall of the basic unit of national identity. It marks the limit of the sacred soil of the motherland. Beyond it lies an alien sovereignty and a foreign citizenship. The boundary in these circumstances is an emotional and psychological divide as well as a geographical line. An unstable nation-state boundary of this category is one which does not coincide with the limits of national identity. The partition of Germany, the separation from France of Alsace-Lorraine, the transfer to Italy from Austria of part of the Tyrol—all these events produced boundaries cutting through regions of cultural and national identity, in the process creating political pressure for boundary change and the reunion of the divided territories. In states where the government is in tune with the national aspirations of the mass of the population, such boundary situations can lead easily enough to crisis and international conflict. No French government, for example, could ever have afforded after 1871 to ignore for long the fact that Germany held Alsace-Lorraine. No government of West Germany today can declare that it has abandoned all hope of reunion with East Germany, even if in practice it may act as if it has done so.

The boundary of a colony may be something rather different. Most of the regions of European colonial expansion involving European rule over non-European majorities were also regions where, at least at the period of colonisation, national sentiment had not reached anything approaching the intensity to be found in the European nation-state. The colonial boundary, in these circumstances, was shaped far more by the needs, strategic or economic, of the colonial power than by the sentiments and aspirations of the colonial populations. Many Asian and African

B

colonial boundaries failed to follow clear ethnic or cultural divides. There was a strong tendency for such boundaries to enclose within one fold groups which had no common tradition of national identity. The colonial powers did not hold colonial boundaries with anything like the same reverence they held the boundaries of their metropolitan territories. There are, of course, exceptions. Russian expansion into Asia, even though it did involve the conquest of non-Russian peoples, was in a very real sense the expansion of the sacred soil of Mother Russia. As a general rule, however, colonial powers had a freedom of action in boundary-making in colonial territories which they did not enjoy at home. It would, for example, have been even more difficult for the Dutch government to hand over a few acres of the Netherlands to Germany or Belgium than it was for the same government to transfer West Irian to Indonesia. No German today resents Australian influence in the former German possessions in New Guinea, but many Germans find it very difficult to reconcile themselves to a permanent partition of Germany. One of the most urgent tasks confronting the independent regime of a former colony is to solve the problem of the boundaries bequeathed to it by the departed imperial power. Where such boundaries in colonial times were not designed to meet the basic requirements of a sovereign nation-state, the independent post-colonial government must inevitably give serious thought to boundary rectification.

A great power, fully conscious of its national identity and aware of the political limits of that identity, may yet show interest beyond its accepted boundaries on grounds of security rather than nationality; for a boundary has a defensive function. Since the sixteenth century, the Channel has formed the southern British boundary. British governments, however, have shown great concern about the nature of the states immediately across the Channel. It used to be an axiom of British policy, for example, that no great continental power should hold the mouth of the Scheldt. Belgium, while beyond doubt outside the British *boundary*, yet formed part of the British *frontier*, as we have defined that term here. In this sense, a great deal of the history of international relations has been concerned with a frontier policy. The Warsaw Pact can be interpreted as an attempt by Russia to create a frontier zone between its own territory and that of the Western alliance; CENTO and SEATO might be seen as Western endeavours to create a frontier zone around the southern edge of the communist world in Asia.

During the great period of European empire-building in Asia, in the nineteenth and early twentieth centuries, British, Russian and French statesmen gave a great deal of thought to frontier policy in this sense. Lord Curzon's 1907 lecture, to which reference has already been made, was but one theoretical expression of such thinking. A large number of categories of frontier situation was analysed, and more than one solution was devised for the defence of the boundary by means of the extension of influence beyond the boundary line. One device was to locate the boundary beyond the line of actual administration, thereby creating a frontier tract into which the potentially hostile influences would find it harder to penetrate, and which could, if the case arose, provide a buffer between two powers which would find it politically expedient not to come into direct administrative contact with each other. There were other ways of building such buffers. A system of protectorates could be erected outside the boundary line. By means of bipartite agreement between the colonial powers, transboundary regions could be divided into spheres of influence or interest: a process which could be accomplished without any reference to the sovereign authorities in the districts involved. Such was the Anglo-Russian partition of Iran in 1907, with the added feature here of a neutral zone between the British and Russian spheres.

Colonial frontier policy, like colonial boundary-making, was a product of the great military and political strength of the colonial powers: a strength in the last analysis derived from the technological advances of the Industrial Revolution. The colonial powers had the might, therefore they assumed the right to carve up Asia and Africa in a manner which suited their own needs but did not of necessity meet the requirements of the Asian and African peoples concerned. This did not matter much to the colonial rulers. The Asian and African peoples under colonial administration or colonial influence did not pose the major threat to the stability of these partitions and divisions; this was to be found in the competition among the colonial powers themselves. The colonial powers, however, had global interests and were not concerned exclusively with the problem of any one region. Anglo-Russian competition in Central Asia could not be divorced from the Balkans and the Eastern Question. Anglo-French rivalry in South-east Asia was related to the colonial partition of Africa. There was a tendency, therefore, to settle the boundary and frontier problems of any one region as part and parcel of a much wider settlement. In 1907, the problem of Tibet was treated in Anglo-Russian negotiations along with the problems of Iran and Afghanistan. This particular combination was rational enough from the point of view of the British and Russians, but it had no logical appeal for the Persians, Afghans or Tibetans.

With the end of the colonial era there also passed away the period when the interests of the colonial powers could decide the pattern of sovereignties in so much of the world. For example, boundaries and frontiers adjusted to the needs of Anglo-Russian diplomacy might not of necessity fulfil the aspirations of independent post-colonial states. It was logical enough to combine Tibet and Afghanistan in a single frontier agreement when both regions touched upon the British Indian empire; but in 1947, with the partition of that empire between India and Pakistan, a quite different situation arose. Pakistan had no common border with Tibet. India had no common border with Afghanistan. Yet both India and Pakistan were to inherit the consequences of what, for them, was obsolete British geopolitical thinking.

In arriving at their frontier settlements, as we have already noted, the colonial powers were often able to ignore many purely local factors. The political evolution of states was arrested or diverted. People who had never been combined before found themselves subjects of the same colony. Sources of tension were thereby created which might only become apparent with the passing of colonial government. Problems arose which could be solved only by a reversal of colonial policy; this has proved to be no easy task because, in many instances, colonial policies and attitudes have been inherited, along with colonial boundaries, by the rulers of the successor states to the colonial empires. We have here, in fact, a three-tiered phenomenon. The European colonial powers when they expanded into Asia found a process at work in the evolution of sovereignties and their limits. The colonial powers checked, exploited or altered the direction of this process. The consequences of the policy of the colonial powers was inherited by their independent successors. To understand the present situation, we cannot afford to confine ourselves exclusively to current history; to do so would be to ignore many major trends which either developed during the colonial period or were masked by colonial policy, and are only now once more beginning to take effect.

★

For the purposes of this study, a rather restricted definition of the term 'Asia' has been used in a quest for geopolitical coherence. The traditional Asia of the geography texts and school atlases includes the Arab states of the Middle and Near East, Iraq, Syria, Jordan, Lebanon and the Arabian peninsula, which cannot today be considered usefully in isolation from Egypt and the Arab countries of North Africa; and it also embraces Turkey east of the Bosphorus: a region which it is not easy to separate from the European Balkans. If these areas are stripped from the

Asian core, and if peripheral archipelagoes like Indonesia and the Philippines are ignored, then there remains what Sir Halford Mackinder described in his classic paper of 1904, *The Geographical Pivot of History*, as the 'pivot area' (or 'heartland' in his revised terminology of 1919) of the Eurasian land mass with

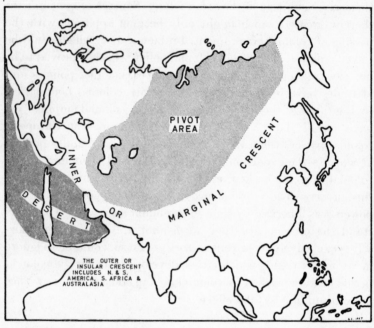

1. Sir Halford Mackinder's 'Pivot Area' or 'Heartland'.

the eastern half of its periphery—what he termed the 'inner or marginal crescent'. (See Map 1.)

What Mackinder, in fact, did in his 1904 paper was to mark out the Asian area of continental and Arctic drainage: the regions where rivers either flowed into inland depressions or into the icy waters of the northern ocean. By this device he combined the Iranian plateau, most of Afghanistan, Tibet, Sinkiang, Mongolia, and the vast expanse of Russian territory from the

Volga basin eastwards to the shores of the Pacific. The resulting region was shaped like an inverted triangle with its base along the shores of the Arctic Ocean and its apex in southern Afghanistan thrusting towards the route which in 1904 still linked British India to southern Iran and the coasts of the Persian Gulf. Here was the sharp end of the 'pivot area' or 'heartland'; and in 1919, at the time of the Versailles peace negotiations, Mackinder declared:

> When our statesmen are in conversation with the defeated enemy, some airy cherub should whisper to them from time to time this saying:
>
> Who rules East Europe commands the Heartland:
> Who rules the Heartland commands the World-Island;
> Who rules the World-Island commands the World.*

On analysis this can be seen to have been a very British observation; for what Mackinder was really saying was that the Russians, by virtue of their peculiarly easy access to the 'heartland', were in a position to threaten the keystone of the British imperial arch, India.

Except in the rather limited context of Anglo-Russian imperial rivalry, Mackinder's theory of the 'heartland' does not really bear serious examination; and its importance is more as an example of a kind of thinking about the interaction of geographical and political factors than as a final geopolitical solution to the problems of Eurasian history. Genghis Khan and Tamerlane may have founded world empires from bases in the 'heartland', but neither they, nor their successors, were able to maintain their power out of the rather limited economic and demographic resources of this region. Empires with a 'heartland' centre have tended to disintegrate into several fragments, each one dominated by a region of settled civilisation outside Mackinder's pivotal zone. His geographical model does not work

* Sir Halford Mackinder, *Democratic Ideals and Reality*, London 1919.

very well in practice. A modification of it, however, may well be useful even if the resulting conclusions may be rather different. Some such modification is attempted here as a framework within which to consider the nature and the evolutionary history of land frontiers and boundaries in the Asian continent.

A glance at the map of the Asian continent as it has been

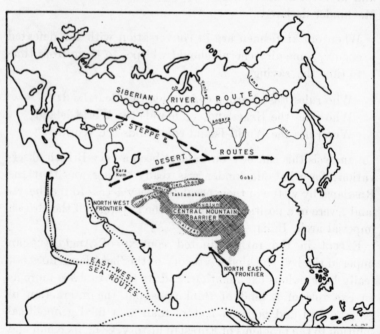

2. Major lines of communication in the Asian landmass.

defined here, that is to say without Turkey, the Arab world and the Arabian peninsula, and the outer island groups, will show six main features. (See Map 2.) First: right across the extreme north of the Asian land mass from the Urals to the Pacific lies the zone of forest and tundra which is the drainage basin of rivers flowing into the Arctic. The upper reaches of these rivers lie sufficiently close to each other to provide a system of waterways leading from the Volga basin in European Russia all the way to the Sea of Okhotsk. Here is the extreme northern route between East and West which was exploited with extraordinary speed by the Russians in the late sixteenth and early seventeenth centuries.

Second: to the south of the basins of the Arctic rivers lies another trans-Asian highway, that of the steppe system linking Manchuria to the eastern fringes of Central Europe. This was the great road of nomad movement, used from the earliest times of which there exists any record and only closed in the modern age of political evolution based on the technology of the Industrial Revolution. The steppe route was amply provided with southward-leading subsidiary roads. Thus, a nomad power with its original base in Mongolia—like that of the Mongols of Genghis Khan—could move out from the steppe system to penetrate China, north-west India, Iran, the Levant and Eastern Europe. The existence of such roads, however, while making access possible, did not result in the permanent combination of these diverse regions into a world state. The steppe system linked stable power centres; it was not, except for brief periods, a stable power centre in its own right.

Third: south of the steppe system, and near the apex of the inverted triangle of Mackinder's 'heartland', lies a most formidable region of mountains and deserts. Three major desert regions—those of the Gobi, the Taklamakan and Transcaspia—line the southern flank of the steppe road. All can be circumvented or crossed with varying degrees of difficulty, but all serve to increase the problems of building political links across them between the steppe system and the centres of settled civilisation to their south. Throughout history, at least until the advances in transportation created by the Industrial Revolution, these deserts have served as an insulation between the steppe and the southern maritime tracts of Asia.

Fourth: south of the deserts lies an even more formidable barrier, that of the mountain system of the Tibetan plateau and its flanking ranges extending both eastwards and west-wards. These mountains stretch from the northern mainland of South-east Asia and western China on the one hand to the Hindu Kush in central Afghanistan on the other. Their central reach outlined by the Himalayas is, at least from the point of view of the broad sweep of history, impassable. Elsewhere—in Yunnan and Burma, in the Karakoram, the Pamirs and the Hindu Kush and its outlying ranges—there exist passes which have performed important roles in the saga of population movement and empire-building. Thus, the mountain system, reinforced to a considerable extent by the deserts to its north, has tended to deflect historical pressures from its centre to its eastern and western edges. The result has been to create a wheel-like geopolitical structure with the Tibetan plateau as its hub. Nothing comes across Tibet; everything goes around it.

Fifth: around the periphery of the southern half of this wheel with its mountainous hub lie three main regions of settled civilisation separated from each other by transitional zones. To the east is China, stretching in a crescent from the edge of the steppe system in Manchuria and Mongolia to the hills and fertile river valleys of the South-east Asian mainland. In the centre is the Indian subcontinent, the home of Hindu culture, flanked by mainland South-east Asia on the east and by the Afghan highland on the west. In the west is Iran, another centre of a distinctive civilisation based on settled agriculture and urban life. To the north, Iran, by way of the oasis cities of Turkestan, is linked to the steppe system. To the east, Iran overflows into the valley of the Indus river and its tributaries. There have been periods in history—the age of the Mongol and Timurid empires from the thirteenth to the sixteenth centuries provides an example—when all three of these major civilisation centres round the southern side of the mountain hub have been affected by the same broad historical forces. In general, how-ever, the presence of the mountain hub has severely limited regional interactions. If we regard the mountain hub and its rim, the steppe road on the north and the peripheral civilisations on its south, as a single major geopolitical system, then for much of its history that system has operated as if it were an assemblage of unconnected subsystems. One such subsystem would be that linking Turkestan, Iran and north-west India, another would involve north-east India, mainland South-east Asia and western China, and yet another China and the eastern end of the steppe world. Much of Asian frontier history has developed within the framework of these subsystems rather than as a product of the operation of the major system as a single entity.

Sixth: the civilisations of Iran, the Indian subcontinent and China are linked to their south by another road which in modern times has acquired an importance quite as great as that of the steppe road. The Indian and Pacific oceans, joined by the Malacca Straits, provide a sea route which was already of commercial significance by the early years of the Christian era and which, in the sixteenth century, became the channel which brought European political influence to the coasts of the Asian mainland. In time, the technology of sea power provided the base on which were founded the British empire in India and the French empire in Indochina. Many of the frontier and boundary problems of modern Asia derive from the disintegration of these colonial regimes established and maintained by sea.

The rise of the colonial empires in Asia makes it possible to describe the Asian geopolitical system, the wheel with the mountains at its hub, in another way. Three main zones can be defined. First: there is the Russian Zone, the area of Russian rule first established along the extreme northern road of the Siberian rivers and then extended, directly or indirectly, over the greater part of the steppe system. Second: there is the Southern Zone, the region of Iran, the Indian subcontinent and mainland South-east Asia which saw the rise of French and British imperial rule and influence based, in the last analysis, on control over the great southern sea road of the Indian and

Pacific oceans. Third: there is the Chinese Zone, the political and cultural sphere of China which was subjected to intense colonial pressure in the nineteenth and twentieth centuries but which, by 1950, had managed to survive with its essential core

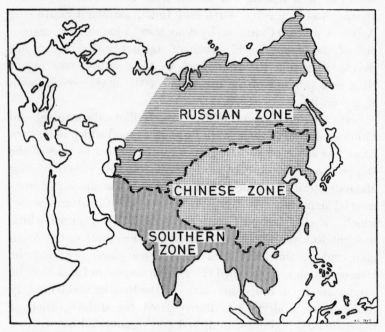

RUSSIAN ZONE

CHINESE ZONE

SOUTHERN ZONE

3. The three zones: the major geopolitical divisions employed in this study.

intact. These zones divide the Asian wheel into three segments, with much of the hub falling within the Chinese Zone. (See Map 3.) The major frontier problems of Asia lie in the definition of the lines of demarcation between these three zones: problems which, in many cases, have their origins in periods long before the age of the great colonial empires.

PART I

Pre-Colonial and Imperial Eras

I

Chinese Frontiers in the Pre-Colonial Era

No state in Asia has a longer land frontier than China, and no state in Asia has been concerned with problems of frontier policy over a longer period. For more than 2,000 years, the history of Chinese intentions and actions on the frontier has been recorded in considerable detail. Modern Chinese statesmen know what their predecessors did under dynasties which flourished before the opening of the Christian era. As a consequence of the remarkable amplitude of Chinese literary sources combined with the persistence of Chinese governmental traditions, China exhibits a continuity of frontier policy which is not to be found elsewhere in Asia.

The Chinese state had its origins along the middle reaches of the Hwang Ho, and it has taken more than three millennia for it to attain the present extent of its domination. During this period it had to face three basic categories of frontier problem. First: from the outset, the centres of Chinese civilisation were extremely vulnerable to attack by nomad groups from the steppe lands of Central Asia, groups which the Chinese generally managed to absorb into their cultural world but at a considerable

political price. Second: as the sphere of Chinese civilisation
expanded, it embraced peripheral peoples, some of them ethnically distinct from the Han Chinese. We can see a long history
of this process towards the south and south-west and the
fringes of what are now the states of mainland South-east Asia;
and it is a process which, it can well be argued, is still going on.
Finally, there have been brief periods in Chinese history when
the ruling dynasty gave thought to the possibility of expanding
beyond the limits of the sea frontier; and, of course, in colonial
times, in the nineteenth and twentieth centuries, that same
sea frontier was seen to be as threatened by foreign penetration
as the Central Asian border had been in periods of peak nomad
activity. The sea frontier, though of enormous importance to
modern Chinese strategic thinking, falls outside the limits
which have been set for this study; it will be discussed only
incidentally here. (See Map 4.)

For most of the long period of recorded Chinese history, it
has been the Central Asian border—what Owen Lattimore, in a
classic analysis, has termed the 'Inner Asian' frontier—which
has posed the greatest danger to the security of the Chinese
state.* It should cause no surprise, therefore, that Chinese
statesmen both past and present have shown such persistent
concern with this frontier, and that they should have been so
sensitive (at least during times when China was politically
strong and united) to threats from this direction. Without
doubt, the most dramatic demonstration of this fact is to be
found in the Great Wall of China, which runs across the north
of the country from the Gulf of Chihli in the Yellow Sea to the
mountains on the edge of Tibet. The distance in a straight line
between the two termini of the Wall is over 1,000 miles; and

---

* Owen Lattimore, *Inner Asian Frontiers of China*, New York 1951.
The expression 'Inner Asia' is intended to include Manchuria: a region
which, it might be held, does not form part of Central Asia. I have
tended in this book to use, at least in a Chinese context, Central Asia to
cover Manchuria as well as Mongolia, Tibet and Turkestan.

the actual length of the Wall—or, more accurately, a whole series of walls—is considerably greater than this. Work on this defence system began more than two centuries before the opening of the Christian era and continued into modern times. Some of the earlier defence lines are considerably to the north of the

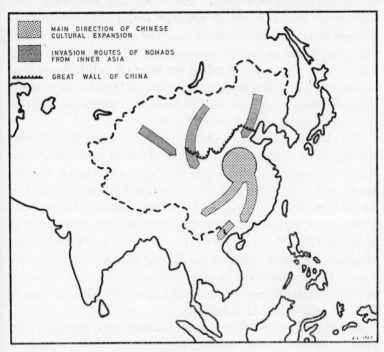

MAIN DIRECTION OF CHINESE CULTURAL EXPANSION

INVASION ROUTES OF NOMADS FROM INNER ASIA

GREAT WALL OF CHINA

4. Main directions of Chinese cultural expansion and of nomad invasions of China.

present Wall—stretches of which, still in excellent repair, lie within fifty miles of Peking, the modern Chinese capital.

The Great Wall, of course, proved in practice to be no more successful than the Maginot Line when attacked by a determined adversary; and no powerful dynasty relied on it as the sole means of defence. It was a patrol line rather than a line

C

held in force throughout its length, but its penetration required large concentrations of forces. While the enemy was assembling to attempt its breach, the Chinese could gain time to make their own preparations along the threatened sector. For much of its history, the Wall system served more as a customs and immigration barrier than as a major line of military resistance; and there were certainly periods when its major task was to keep Chinese in rather than nomads out. The true defence of China depended more on policy and strategy than on engineering works; and, above all, it called for internal political stability and strength in China proper. On this basis, the Chinese evolved another defensive system with its outermost limits well beyond the barrier alignment of the Great Wall.

The historical danger to China across the 'Inner Asian' frontier lay in the formation beyond the Wall of a nomadic confederation sufficiently powerful and aggressive to be able to sweep down into the regions of settled Chinese population. There were many ways in which such a nomad danger could arise; and it did not always strike from the same quarter of the compass. It could, for example, come from the north-west along or across the upper valley of the Hwang Ho; or again, as in the case of the last such successful conquest (that of the Manchus in the seventeenth century), it could come from the north-east, from what is called Manchuria.

Experience proved that the only satisfactory answer to the problem of the Chinese 'Inner Asian' frontier was the establishment beyond it of a zone of Chinese influence. The object of such a policy—at least, until very recent times—was not to convert districts beyond the Wall into Chinese colonies; rather, the intention was to construct a system of bodies politic which would be so controlled by Chinese diplomacy as to be unable or unwilling to act in concert in attacks on Chinese territory. The system might well be laid down by military conquest (as, for example, in the great periods of the Han, T'ang and Ch'ing dynasties), but once established it was in general maintained by methods of diplomacy and indirect rule which could at times produce something not unlike the protectorates of the late nineteenth-century European empires. The system was not designed—at least, not until the very end of the dynastic era— to bring about the integration of the tracts beyond the Wall into the direct administrative structure of China. (See Map 5.)

In effect, what the Chinese traditionally tried to do in the frontier tracts beyond the Wall was to establish a pattern of

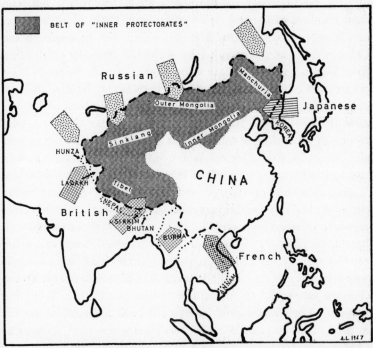

5. The Chinese 'protectorate' system and the main directions of British, French, Russian and Japanese pressure in the late nineteenth and early twentieth centuries. The 'Inner Protectorates' (Tibet, Sinkiang, Inner and Outer Mongolia, Manchuria) are shown as shaded areas within the Chinese border. Some of the 'Outer Protectorates' (like Annam, Burma, Bhutan, Sikkim, Nepal, Ladakh and Hunza are shown outside the Chinese border.

'protectorates', of states which acknowledged some degree of dependency upon the Chinese central government without being under its direct administration. Chinese influence could be exercised in a number of ways: by treaties and dynastic marriage alliances; by the conferring of titles and the payment of subsidies; by the establishment of regional representatives carrying out many of the functions of a Resident in a European colony of indirect rule. Whatever the method employed, the Chinese traditionally maintained a strict separation between their conduct of Central Asian affairs and their administration of China proper. During Manchu times, for example, when China was in fact controlled by a foreign dynasty originating from beyond the Wall, the execution of Inner Asian frontier policy tended to be concentrated in Manchu hands. Chinese officials—that is to say, officials who were members of what is now often called the Han Chinese race and who did not belong to one of the ruling Manchu tribal groups—were as far as possible excluded from Central Asia, even though they were able to rise to the highest ranks of the internal Chinese administration.

The structure of the 'protectorate' system was extremely complex, and any brief description of it will inevitably involve a measure of oversimplification. Analysis is further complicated by the very nature of the traditional Chinese concept of foreign relations, in which all foreign states were seen as being in some way tributary to and dependent on the Chinese dynasty. To the Chinese emperor, all foreign embasies were tribute-bearing missions. Lord Macartney's mission of 1793 is described as such in the Chinese annals. Many of the states which paid 'tribute' to China—some of the South-east Asian kingdoms, for example, or remote mountain districts like Nepal and Hunza—did so in a highly symbolical and sometimes rather indirect manner, and their rulers did not thereby feel themselves seriously inhibited from entering into relationships with states other than China. Other regions, like Mongolia and Tibet, were, at least in periods of Chinese strength, far more restricted in their diplomatic freedom because of their Chinese ties. As one might expect, the Chinese tended to exercise more control over those areas which provided the most obvious and most direct threats to Chinese security.

An essential feature in the Chinese tributary system was that the bringer of tribute should, while in China, receive gifts from the emperor of greater value than his tribute. In other words, while in theory paying to the Chinese, in fact the tributary would be in receipt of some kind of Chinese subsidy. Thus, in periods of Chinese economic and political decline, the tributary system could prove very expensive, and any attempt on the part of the Chinese to reduce their tributary commitments could lead to the apparently paradoxical demands of the tributaries to increase the frequency of their missions. In this respect, the Chinese tributary policy in 'Inner Asia' is not without its parallels elsewhere. Byzantium practised a very similar policy towards its nomadic neighbours, with comparable results in periods of imperial decline in Constantinople.

How did the Chinese regard their Inner Asian tribute-paying 'protectorates'? To what extent were regions like Tibet, Mongolia and Chinese Turkestan considered to be part of China? It seems more than probable that the Chinese, at least until the end of the nineteenth century, maintained in their minds a clear distinction between the tributary areas and China proper. The history of European colonialism reveals two quite distinct approaches to the nature of the sovereignty of colonial possessions. On the one hand, colonies can be viewed as an integral part of the motherland; such are the Russian possessions in Asia and such, in constitutional theory at least, are the colonies of Portugal. On the other hand, there can be injected into colonial theory an element of protection, even of trusteeship, to create a relationship between colonial power and colony which is quite distinct from the relationship between that power and its own metropolitan citizens. The Chinese, had their constitutional philosophy provided room for two such interpretations as these, would probably have applied the latter to their Central Asian 'protectorates', and especially to the remoter districts.

Until the age of the expansion of Europe into Asia, such a distinction, of course, was but academic from the Chinese point of view. The areas of Chinese influence and interest in Central Asia were not threatened by foreign, non-Central Asian powers. The danger to Chinese influence lay within Central Asia where a nomad power could arise to threaten the Chinese heartland as, for example, did the empire of the Mongols in the thirteenth century. The basic interest to China of these Central Asian regions was not as colonies (in the European sense) but as zones of danger for the Chinese heartland. Of course, there were other Chinese interests as well (religious and economic, for example), but these were minor when compared with the question of the defence of the frontier of metropolitan China as symbolised by the line of the Wall. This is a most important point, because it leads to the conclusion that the Chinese were far more concerned with the border between themselves and their Central Asian 'protectorates' than they were with the borders between those 'protectorates' and the rest of the world. A similar interest would apply in the case of borders between nearer and remoter 'protectorates'. Nepal provides a good example of the point in question. At the very end of the eighteenth century, a conflict developed between Nepal and Tibet which resulted in a Chinese intervention to restore the peace. Nepal thereupon was obliged to accept a Chinese tributary status. A few years later, Nepal came into conflict with the British, as a result of which the latter annexed considerable tracts of territory which had been under Nepalese control. The Chinese showed no interest in this process of evolution of an Anglo-Nepalese border, yet they continued to show—and still do so today—a keen interest in the Tibeto-Nepalese border. In other words, the Chinese were more interested, as one would have expected, in the inner limits of their frontier system than they were in its outermost dimensions.

In modern times, under the influence of colonial pressures, some Chinese writers have endeavoured to establish the rightful limits of the Chinese state on the basis of the full extent of the old 'protectorate' system. This has produced claims to vast areas of territory outside the present Chinese boundaries. For example, in *Chung-kuo chin-tai chien-shih* (A Short History of Modern China) edited by Liu P'ei-hua and published in Peking in 1954, it is suggested that China has rights not only to extensive tracts of what is today Russia in Asia, but also to Nepal, Sikkim, Bhutan, Assam, Burma, the Andaman Islands, Malaya, Thailand, Vietnam (North and South), Laos, Cambodia, Taiwan, the Sulu Islands, the Ryukyu Islands and Korea. Other Chinese writers, like Hsieh Pin in his *Chung-kuo sang-ti shih* (A History of China's Lost Territories), published in Shanghai in 1925, make even more extensive claims. (See Map 6.) Claims to territory of this kind, however, have tended to remain theoretical, and they have not, in either Kuomintang or Communist times, formed the basis for official Chinese frontier policy.

Geography, of course, provided a theoretical maximum limit to the area of the Chinese 'protectorates' of Central Asia. The Himalayas, the Karakoram, the Pamirs and the Tien Shan mountain ranges were formidable barriers, as were also the Siberian forests and tundra to the north of Mongolia and Manchuria. There were times when the Chinese did extend their influence beyond some of these natural barriers (in both the Han and the Manchu periods, for example, there was Chinese military penetration into the Pamirs, in what is now Russian territory); but these were brief episodes. The broad limits of the Chinese sphere were clear enough, at least to the traditional Chinese scholar-administrator. Chinese Turkestan, Tibet, Mongolia, Manchuria, Korea: these were the frontier zones of the Chinese world; and a strong and secure China would have to have some influence over the course of events in these regions. The exact nature of that influence, however, and the precise extent of the region in which it was to be exercised, inevitably varied with time and circumstance.

The Chinese view of the proper position of Central Asia in the world order was not always shared by the Central Asian peoples themselves. While the Tibetans, Uighurs, Mongols, Manchus and the like, in the course of a long history of contact, acquired

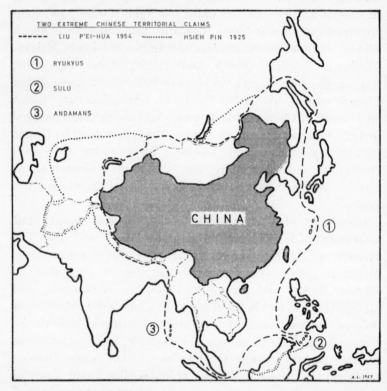

6. Two extreme views as to the rightful limits of Chinese territory before the imperialist advance. These borders represent the limits of the Chinese tributary system as taken to theoretical extremes. Some Kazakh groups, for example, had entered into tributary relations with the Manchus; therefore the extreme theory argues that the entire area of Kazakh population should be Chinese.

a certain predisposition to look upon China as the centre of the civilised world (much as the Germanic peoples considered Rome to be), yet the bulk of the Central Asian populations did not become Sinicised. It was not the traditional Chinese policy to turn Uighurs into Chinese; indeed, there existed a strong tendency to impose restrictions on the expansion of Chinese culture beyond the Wall. Moreover, there were long periods when the Central Asian regions passed right out of the Chinese sphere. From the Central Asian point of view, the tie with China did not appear either so desirable or so essential on strategic grounds as it did to the Chinese scholar-statesmen with ready access to the histories of the great dynasties.

Some of the regions of Central Asia which the Chinese saw as falling within their sphere also possessed strong ties with centres of civilisation right outside the limits of the Chinese world. During the first millennium of the Christian era, Buddhism spread northwards from India into Turkestan and Tibet. From that period Tibet retained a measure of cultural contact with the Buddhist homeland to the south, though this was to be restricted greatly by the expansive force of Islam which, between the eighth and thirteenth centuries, established its domination over Afghanistan and the northern Indian plains. Islam did not penetrate into Tibet, but in Turkestan it replaced Buddhism as the dominant religion, thereby linking the oasis cities of the Tarim basin with the Muslim world to the west.

Tendencies leading to an orientation away from China were reinforced by the history of Central Asian empires arising in periods of Chinese weakness. For example, the Mongol empire in the thirteenth century not only linked China to Central Asia but also extended Central Asian power westwards into Iran, Mesopotamia and Eastern Europe. Such empires, of which the Mongols provide an extreme example, not only fostered traditions of Central Asian independence but also, in their decline, broke up into successor states which sometimes straddled sections of the line of the natural limits of the Chinese sphere.

A large number of factors, of which some only have been sketched here in outline, combined to produce three major features in the history of the Chinese frontier in Central Asia. First: Chinese influence in Central Asia tended not only to be indirect but also to be unstable. There were periods in Chinese history when the entire Inner Asian frontier zone—more than a million square miles in area—passed right out of Chinese control. If we take the Chinese boundary to be the line defining the extent of Chinese political influence, however indirectly applied, then that line was subject to fluctuations of gargantuan proportions. Second: it was often extremely difficult to define the precise limits of the Chinese sphere. While the demarcation between China proper and Inner Asia might be clear and sharp, yet the external limits of Inner Asia might be extremely vague. Finally: the Chinese were not particularly concerned with the outer limits of Inner Asia so long as no real threats to Chinese security could be detected beyond those limits.

At first sight, a number of close parallels might be found between the traditional pattern of Chinese policy towards the Inner Asian zone and that towards mainland South-east Asia. In both regions we can see the Chinese endeavouring to extend their influence beyond their metropolitan borders by means of a system of 'protectorates' and tributary relationships. A closer examination, however, shows that there are fundamental differences between the Inner Asian and South-east Asian Chinese land borders, both in the manner of their evolution and the conduct of Chinese policy towards them.

The first point, of course, is that China in the pre-European period was never seriously threatened by invasion from the south and the south-west as it was from the north and the north-east. Mainland South-east Asia produced its share of empires. The Khmers, for example, with their capital in the Angkor region, dominated most of what is today Cambodia and Thailand at the moment when the Mongol empire of Genghis Khan was being born. Unlike the Mongols, however, the Khmers did not have it in their power to establish anything like world dominion. They could never have founded a Chinese dynasty as did the successors of Genghis Khan. Even a clearly expansionist South-east Asian state, like that of the Konbaung dynasty of Burma in the late eighteenth and early nineteenth centuries, posed no more than an incidental challenge to Chinese power in peripheral regions. The Manchus waged a series of extremely unsuccessful campaigns against Burma in 1766–69, but their failure in no way threatened the Manchu hold on metropolitan China. The Manchu emperor, Ch'ien Lung, certainly did not regard Burman politics with anything like the alarm that he showed towards developments among the Dzungars of Central Asia at just about the same period. In Peking, the Dzungars were seen as a menace of the classic type while the Burmans were not.

The spread of Chinese civilisation south of the Yangtze towards what is now mainland South-east Asia was a slow process of cultural absorption as well as military conquest. It was most rapid along the south China coast, where, by the end of the third century BC, it had brought the power of the Ch'in dynasty—the first, though short-lived, dynasty to rule over a united Chinese state—into the Red River delta, in what is today North Vietnam.* China's expansion into Yunnan towards the borders of modern Burma and Laos took much longer to accomplish, and, indeed, could be said to have been still going on in the nineteenth century. This advance to the south-west from the outset involved the expansion of the Chinese provincial structure. Such an expansion was possible because it embraced populations which were capable of being absorbed into the world of Chinese civilisation. This factor of proneness to Sinicisation was probably as much political and economic as it was ethnic or linguistic. The populations of the

* But it should be noted that at this early period Vietnam, and, indeed, adjacent tracts to its north, were treated as 'commanderies', as marcher districts, rather than as an integral part of China proper.

rice plains of the Red River delta in Vietnam or the Tali region
of Yunnan were an obvious field for the expansion of administra-
trative techniques already developed in similar environments
under Chinese control. Failing the presence of any alternative
form of sophisticated governmental structure, such districts on
the fringes of the Chinese world would inevitably follow the
Chinese model, either by imitation or by imposition. Far slower,
on the other hand, would be the advance of Chinese government and civilisation into the hill tracts where tribal peoples
followed a way of life alien to the pattern of settled Chinese
rural and urban society. Here was far less fertile soil for the
proliferation of *hsien*, the magistrate's districts of imperial
China.

The first phase of Chinese expansion towards South-east
Asia—what one scholar has called 'China's march towards the
tropics'—took place at a period when another civilisation was
also expanding its influence into the South-east Asian mainland.
By the beginning of the Christian era, political and religious
ideas of Indian origin were crossing the Bay of Bengal. The
origins of this process and the nature of its early stages remain
obscure. Of the result, however, there can be little doubt. In
Burma, Thailand, Cambodia, southern Vietnam and the Malay
peninsula, as well as in the Indonesian islands, there emerged
the nuclei of an Indianised civilisation capable of developing
governmental structures resistant to Chinese absorption. This
was to be of fundamental importance in the history of the evolution of China's land border in the south-west, for, with one
great exception, this border represents a divide between the
cultural influences of India and China.

The great exception is to be found in Vietnam. The Viets,
with their original home in the Red River delta in what is now
North Vietnam, remained within the Chinese cultural sphere
even though, unlike other groups in Yunnan, Kwangsi and
Kwangtung, they managed to resist permanent Chinese political
absorption. They were but little affected by the Indian-

influenced cultures of their South-east Asian neighbours, though the process of the expansion of the Viet state from Tonkin towards the Mekong delta in the south involved the conquest of Indianised groups like the Chams. The Viets were obvious targets for absorption by China, and on more than one occasion the Chinese attempted to swallow them up. The Chinese, however, failed. The Viets, though highly Sinicised, yet maintained a national identity strong enough to enable them to retain their political independence. Thus, they became a buffer between south-west China and the Indianised states of the Mekong valley. Vietnam still performs this role today, which goes far to explain its place in Western geopolitical thought.

With China's expansion to the south-west, mainland South-east Asia inevitably turned into a frontier zone in which the Chinese state from time to time endeavoured to establish some measure of influence. For example, during the latter part of the thirteenth century, the Chinese rulers—at this period the Yuan dynasty, the Mongol successors to Genghis Khan—launched attacks against the Viets and Chams of the Indochinese peninsula and the Burmans of the Irrawaddy valley. The Mongols, moreover, did not confine themselves to the mainland; Kubilai Khan even attempted an abortive conquest of Java in the Indonesian archipelago. These Mongol operations in South-east Asia were devastating in their local consequences in that they shattered established powers and paved the way for the rise of new states and the dominance of the region by new groups. They did not, however, lead to permanent Chinese conquest, and they were quite uncharacteristic of the general pattern of Chinese policy towards the south-west. They took place at a unique period when China, under foreign rule, formed part of an empire which at its height stretched from the Mediterranean to the Pacific. More characteristic of Chinese policy was the creation of dependent relationships between the major South-east Asian powers and Peking. During Ming and Manchu

times, most of the major powers of the South-east Asian mainland became the subject of Chinese diplomacy. In Chinese eyes
the Burmans, the Thais, the Viets, the Malays of the Malacca
sultanate—all were seen as tributaries to China. The relationship, however, was in the main confined to symbols and had but
slight consequences for the internal politics of the regions
involved. Mainland South-east Asia, unlike Central Asia, posed
no threat to the integrity and security of the Chinese state.

Until very recent times, indeed, mainland South-east Asia
was in one respect the very reverse of Central Asia. In the latter
region, nomad confederations provided the foundation for
attacks on the Chinese heartland. Tribal developments along
the fringes of south-west China, on the other hand, could have
the gravest consequences for the history of mainland South-east
Asia. From the earliest times, so archæological and anthropo-
logical evidence has suggested, this area was penetrated by
groups of peoples migrating from south and south-west China.
Some authorities assign a Chinese origin to the neolithic populations of both mainland and island South-east Asia. For more
recent times, we have good evidence of the movement south-
westwards of peoples like the Burmans, Thais, Shans and Laos
who between the eighth and thirteenth centuries of our era
seem to have moved out of what today would be Yunnan and
where their relatives can still be found. This process of migration has gone on up to modern times. Some of the hill tribes of
northern Thailand, for example, crossed over from Yunnon
province within living memory, and still speak a Yunnanese
dialect.

The pattern of political evolution in mainland South-east
Asia has been dominated by this process. The centres of Indianised civilisation in the valleys of the great rivers—the Irrawaddy, the Menam and the Mekong—were able to absorb
culturally successive waves of migrant peoples. Between these
centres, however, and the outposts of the Chinese world, there
existed a belt of non-Indianised peoples who occupied a frontier

zone between China and South-east Asia. This zone stretched through hill tracts from the Gulf of Tonkin to the Tibetan plateau. Within it lay a confused pattern of sovereignties through which ran no boundary line to compare with the line of the Great Wall. The creation of a boundary through this frontier was the product of colonial and post-colonial times. The result was no clear ethnic divide.

A distribution map of the non-Chinese minority groups living in western and south-western China provides a fascinating mosaic. Numerically, the most important are those speaking languages of the Thai family, like the Chuang of Kweichow and Kwangsi provinces, and the Lü, Nua and Shan of Yunnan province. There are perhaps 10 million such people in China, making a population about one-third the size of the Thai-speaking population of Thailand. Scattered along the Yunnan side of the Burmese border are groups speaking Tibeto-Burman languages related to Burmese. These include the Lolo tribes, the Lisu, the Lahu and the Minchia, the last numbering more than 600,000 and occupying the Mekong valley north of Tali. Also along the Burmese border in Yunnan are to be found Mon-Khmer speakers like the Wa tribes. Pockets of speakers of both Mon-Khmer and Tibeto-Burman languages are to be found in the hill tracts along the Laotian border of Yunnan. All these minorities have close relatives living outside China in Burma, Laos, Thailand and Vietnam.

Today, apart from the tribal groups referred to above, there are a number of significant Chinese communities resident in South-east Asian states. These overseas Chinese have tended, of late, to be seen as potential fifth columns, the forerunners of a Chinese political expansion south-westwards. In fact, however, the overseas settlement of the Chinese has very little to do with Chinese official frontier policy. The great majority of the Chinese now resident in South-east Asia, both island and main-land, came as traders, miners, labourers and the like, and came on their own initiative. This process has been going on for a long

time, at least since the Sung dynasty (c. AD 1000–1200). Sometimes it took place in explicit defiance of official Chinese policy.
The Mac dynasty, for example, which established itself in the
extreme south of Vietnam in the seventeenth century, owed its
origins to Chinese refugees from the Manchus following the
defeat of the Ming dynasty.* Unlike the tribal groups, the overseas Chinese did not concentrate along the Chinese land borders.
They followed the sea lanes and tended to create Chinese
minority communities in sea ports and commercial centres.
They were not the spearhead of Chinese territorial advance into
South-east Asia; and there is no evidence to suggest that
Chinese officialdom ever considered them as such, at least until
very recent times.

* Mac Cuu, fleeing from the Manchu conquerors of the Chinese Ming
dynasty, established himself in the region of Hatien on what was then
Cambodian soil. Hatien is situated in the extreme south of the Mekong
delta region, in what is now South Vietnam. In the late seventeenth
century it was a meeting place for pirates and adventurers. Mac Cuu
acquired from the Cambodian authorities a gambling concession, which
rapidly brought him great wealth. He was joined by other Chinese
refugees and settlers, and soon he became a territorial magnate, the
governor of Hatien. Throughout the eighteenth century, Mac Cuu's
descendants played an important part in Cambodian and Vietnamese
politics; but at no time did they act as agents or partisans of the Chinese
state. Groups like the Mac dynasty, therefore, cannot be interpreted as
the spearhead of an official Chinese expansionist policy. In time, they
tended to become absorbed into the Indianised world of mainland
South-east Asia by a process of cultural adaptation and intermarriage.
There was, for example, a strong Chinese ethnic element amongst the
founders of the present Thai ruling dynasty, yet it cannot be said that
the Bangkok kingdom today is in any way Chinese in outlook.

2

Early Frontier History in the Southern Zone

That area which has been defined as the Southern Zone can be subdivided conveniently enough into three main regions. First: there is a tract comprising mainland South-east Asia and the north-east corner of the Indian subcontinent. This we may term the eastern edge. Second: there is the bulk of the subcontinent with its northern sector defined by the Himalayan range and the states of Nepal, Sikkim and Bhutan. Finally: there is the north-west sector of the subcontinent, combined with Afghanistan, eastern Iran and portions of Russian and Chinese Turkestan—the zone's north-west corner. The whole zone is far more varied and complex in its frontier history than either the Chinese or Russian zones. It represented the major field of British and French colonial activity in Asia. On the passing of the colonial empires, it has fragmented into a number of fully independent states, like Pakistan, Afghanistan, India, Nepal, Burma, Laos, Cambodia and the two Vietnams. The Southern Zone is at present dominated by no single indigenous power, the Indian republic having so far failed in its efforts to assume the geopolitical mantle of the British Raj.

D

THE EASTERN EDGE

The early history of the eastern edge of the Southern Zone was dominated by the movement of tribal groups southwards and westwards from south-west China and its frontier region. Some of these groups were non-Chinese, speakers of Sino-Thai, Tibeto-Burman or Mon-Khmer languages, who had been only slightly, if at all, influenced by the civilisation of metropolitan China. Among the most Sinicised were the Viets, who had a long history of relations with and rule by China. Other groups, such as Burmans, Shans, Thais and Laos, when they first come on to the stage of recorded South-east Asian history, seem not to have been clad in Chinese robes, as it were; though there can be little doubt that in Yunnan there had existed states controlled by such peoples (the Nanchao kingdom is probably the best-known example), which were to some extent modelled on Chinese patterns of administration. Such states marked, in fact, a frontier zone into which China, both culturally and politically, was expanding. It is reasonable to suppose that the pressure of Chinese expansion was a major factor in the precipitation of migration into South-east Asia. (See Map 7.)

Peoples like the Burmans and the Thais are now looked upon in the West as being indigenous to South-east Asia. It is not generally known that they came to the region as colonisers, often establishing a minority rule over subject peoples whom they had conquered. The process of colonisation was not accomplished overnight—and in many parts of South-east Asia it still goes on. The Burmans have yet to establish absolute authority over the Chins and Karens. The Thais are still endeavouring to absorb Malay peoples south of the Isthmus of Kra. It was in quite modern times that the Viets completed the task of military conquest of the Chams, an Indianised people speaking a Malayo-Polynesian language.

These groups penetrated areas where an Indianised civilisation had already been established; culturally, they were to be profoundly influenced by their conquests. Newly arrived groups,

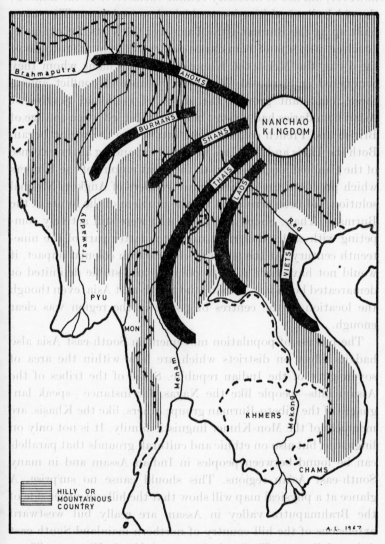

7. The Chinese south-west frontier, showing some of the major tribal movements into South-east Asia in the centuries immediately before the opening of the European colonial era.

however, did not of necessity confine themselves to the limits of the old Indianised kingdoms which they took over. The states built up by the Burmans, the Thais and the Viets, for example, acquired patterns of boundaries rather different from those of the Pyus, the Mons, the Khmers and the Chams whom they conquered or displaced. Moreover, because of conflict among these immigrant groups, the shape of mainland South-east Asian boundaries had not yet become stabilised when the age of British and French colonial penetration into the region began. Both the Thais and the Viets were still expanding at the expense of the Cambodians, the heirs to the great empire of the Khmers which produced the archæological wonders of Angkor. No final solution had been arrived at for the problem of the limits of the Burmans, Thais, Shans and Laos, who were still actively competing with each other right up to the latter part of the nineteenth century. At the moment of European colonial impact, it would not have been easy to point to any stable delimited or demarcated boundary in mainland South-east Asia, even though the location of the centres of power in the region was clear enough.

The process of population movement in South-east Asia also had its effect on districts which are now within the area of sovereignty of the Indian republic. Some of the tribes of the Assam hills—people like the Nagas, for instance—speak languages of the Tibeto-Burman group; others, like the Khasis, are members of the Mon-Khmer linguistic family. It is not only on linguistic, but also on ethnic and cultural, grounds that parallels can be found between peoples in Indian Assam and in many South-east Asian regions. This should cause no surprise. A glance at a physical map will show that the hills on either side of the Brahmaputra valley in Assam are really but westward extensions of the hill country of northern mainland South-east Asia, of Burma, Thailand, Laos and North Vietnam. These hills also extend deep into the Chinese province of Yunnan, and through them runs the tribal belt to which reference was made at the end of the previous chapter. The tribal belt, because of geography, flows over into the north-east corner of the Indian subcontinent and within it there has been a history of population movement extending back far into prehistoric times.

The nature of the South-east Asian frontier is apparent to anyone who, with some experience of the tribal cultures of any of the major regions, undertakes a journey overland from, let us say, Calcutta to the Chittagong hills in East Pakistan. From Calcutta to Dacca, the road crosses the great alluvial plain of the combined streams of the Ganges and the Brahmaputra. The land is completely flat, cut through by countless rivers, and inhabited by peasant cultivators who, though at the East Pakistan border they may change in religion from Hindu to Muslim, yet remain typical of the way of life of the great plains of the northern part of the Indian subcontinent. We might, perhaps, term this the Indo-Gangetic way of life. For a few miles eastward of Dacca this life continues; then, abruptly, the plain comes to an end in a line of low hills. Where the plain penetrates the hills, one still finds tongues of Indo-Gangetic life. The hills themselves, however, are inhabited by tribal groups who are quite different, making artifacts and practising a manner of cultivation which would not seem out of place in northern Thailand or, even, in Borneo or the Philippines. This line of hills, which when one first meets them are but 200 or 300 feet high at the most, represents the natural western frontier of mainland South-east Asia. In the north of Assam, it merges with the frontier hills of Tibet, to the great complication of the process of modern boundary evolution in this region.

In the course of history this westward extension of the South-east Asian mainland has had its political consequences. For instance, at the same time that the Thais and Shans were establishing themselves in South-east Asia, in the late twelfth and early thirteenth centuries, the Ahoms—a group closely related to them both—undertook the conquest of Assam, moving westward down from the hills into the Brahmaputra valley; 1229

is the traditional date for the foundation of the Ahom kingdom
of Assam. This kingdom was to endure, though increasingly
influenced by Indo-Aryan civilisation, until the early nineteenth
century when it came under Burman control, thus provoking
British annexation and the removal of the region, as it were,
from South-east to South Asia. During the Second World War,
the Japanese, following along paths beaten out by the Ahoms
and the Burmans, attempted to reverse this step by the conquest of the Indian subcontinent from a South-east Asian base.
The Japanese 'March on Delhi' was halted in Manipur and the
Naga hills of Assam, but not before it had been demonstrated
that the established line of colonial demarcation between
British Burma and British India was by no means impenetrable. The present eastern boundary of the Indian subcontinent
is not defended by the inexorable laws of geography.

THE NORTHERN LIMITS

In the Indian subcontinent, urban civilisation was flourishing
nearly one millennium before it appears to have begun in China.
Mohenjodaro and Harappa of the Indus valley civilisation are
considerably older than Anyang and other such sites in the
valley of the Hwang Ho. The Indus valley civilisation—based,
it would seem, on a non-Aryan population and with affinities, it
has been conjectured, with the Dravidians of modern south
India—came to an end in about 1500 BC, perhaps because of
climatic or other natural factors, or perhaps in the face of
invasion by Aryan tribes from the Iranian plateau. Though the
archæological record seems to point to a time-gap of many
centuries between the end of the Indus cities and the begin-
nings of Indo-Aryan urban life, literary traditions attest to
more than 3,500 years of continuous Indo-Aryan cultural evolution. Thus, the indigenous contemporary civilisation of the subcontinent is of an antiquity comparable with that of China. The
subcontinent has produced two of the great world religions,
Hinduism and Buddhism, both of which have exercised their

influence far beyond the land and sea frontiers of the region: in Central Asia, China, Japan and South-east Asia. Yet the Indian subcontinent, unlike China, failed in pre-colonial times to evolve into a stable united state: a factor of great importance for the study of the frontier problems of the region.

The unification of China, first achieved in the third century BC, established a pattern for the future. There were to be periods when China would disintegrate into a number of separate, and often conflicting, regimes; but the trend was always towards reunification. The process in India worked in the opposite direction. The creation of empires embracing the greater part of the subcontinent—like that of Mauryas under Asoka in the third century BC or that of the Moghuls which was established during the course of the sixteenth century—did not result in a lasting concept of Indian unity. They were of short life: brief episodes in a long history of a plurality of distinct regional identities. It can be argued with some force that the united India which we see today was far less the product of cultural or political tradition than of European colonial policy.

Many of the divisive forces in Indian society and polity remain despite the consequences of the British Raj. The caste system, which tends to break society up into a large number of separate, inward-looking groups, has shown great powers of resistance in the face of official endeavours to remove some of its more disruptive or degrading effects. The importance of regional language groups in political identity has not been eliminated by the establishment of a central government in New Delhi. Modern prophets of doom find much evidence upon which to base their conclusion that the Indian republic will inevitably break up into a number of nations, each based on language, region, caste or tribe. It may well be that India will become again what it so often was in the past, a land of many boundaries. As it is, more than a century of unity under British rule did not suffice to prevent the partition of the British Indian empire between India and Pakistan.

For our present purpose, the major significance of the divisive forces which have been a perennial factor in the political history of the Indian subcontinent lies in its failure to produce anything like the tradition of frontier policy which developed in China. When the Chinese today speak of the traditional frontiers of their state, they have a very clear idea, based on impressive documentary evidence, of just what they mean. The modern Indian concept of frontier traditions is much more vague. There are great problems to be faced in an attempt to seek out a definition of the term 'India' which antedates the British Raj. The British were not the first foreign rulers of Indian soil. For so much of Indian history, the subcontinent was divided up into a complex pattern of warring states. Some of the difficulties involved in a definition of the 'traditional' (that is to say pre-British) boundary of India can be deduced from a study of the Indian arguments in the Sino-Indian boundary dispute.

In the Sino-Indian discussions of 1960, the Chinese did not find fault with the Indian contention that the Himalayan range represented the frontier of the subcontinent. They disputed, however, and with some reason, that a precise boundary had ever been defined along much of the Himalayan tracts involved; and they pointed out that Indian arguments, particularly those invoking the sanctity of watersheds, had not proved the existence of such a line. What the Chinese were, in effect, saying (though it must be admitted that they did so with a singular lack of tact or consideration), was that much of the Himalayas was still a frontier zone rather than a region of delimited or demarcated boundary lines. There is a great deal of truth in this contention. The fluctuating nature of Indian political evolution in the plains had failed to bring about a sharp divide between the world of the subcontinent and that of the Tibetan plateau. At times Tibetan political influence—to which, of course, the Chinese now laid claim as the heirs to the Lhasa authorities—had expanded southward towards the Himalayan foothills and the edge of the plains. At other times, the influence of states in the plains had penetrated northwards along valleys leading to the Himalayan crests. There were stretches of the Himalayan frontier zone in Assam which had been but super-ficially influenced, if at all, by either north or south, and which were, to all intents and purposes, no-man's-lands.

In some ways, the Himalayan frontier of the Indian sub-continent resembled the South-east Asian frontier of China. It marked a zone of buffer territories across which existed no threat of major invasion.* The history of the Indian sub-continent, like that of China, is very much dominated by the recurrent theme of foreign attack. The danger, however, did not lie in the north. The Himalayas, though passed easily enough by small groups and through which ran trade routes and roads along which spread cultural influences, were an effective enough barrier against large armies. No Indian state ever maintained a lasting domination over the Tibetan plateau. No power based on this area has ever established lasting control over the plains south of the Himalayas. The major threat to Indian security from the earliest period of which we have any knowledge, the classic invasion route, lay along the western edge of the Indian basin across what in British times came to be known as the North-West Frontier.

THE NORTH-WEST CORNER

The North-West Frontier has long been regarded as the tradi-tional invasion route into the Indian subcontinent. From this

* Until a British army marched to Lhasa in 1904, the only recorded major Indian campaign directed beyond the Himalayan crests was that of one of the Delhi sultans in the fourteenth century. It ended in disaster. The various Gurkha attacks on Tibet in the eighteenth and nineteenth centuries were all launched from a base within the Himalayan range. They were certainly no major threat to the security of the Chinese empire. India, at least until 1962, has never been seriously threatened by major attacks from Tibetan bases; though the British argued, rather unconvincingly, that a danger of this kind might develop if the Russians were allowed to make contact with the Dalai Lama—hence the British military mission to Tibet in 1940.

direction in the second millennium BC came the Aryan tribes to
overthrow—so some scholars think—the old cities of the Indus
valley and to lay the foundations of the civilisation of the
Hindus. Other peoples followed in the Aryan footsteps. The
Achæmenian empire of Persia in the age of Cyrus, Darius and
Xerxes endeavoured to maintain a satrapy along the Indus.
The Achæmenian example was followed by its successors, the
regime of Alexander the Great, the Greek kings of Bactria, the
Parthians and the Sassanians. There was barely a century
between the opening of the Christian era and the creation of
British India in the nineteenth century when some force, great
or small, did not fight its way down to the Indian plains from
the Afghan highlands across the passes of the North-West
Frontier. Sakas, Kushans, Huns, Turks and Pathans in turn
contributed to the disruption of Indian society by external
attack. Islam was brought to India from the north-west by
invading Arab or Turk armies; and the history of the Islamic
Delhi sultanate, from its foundation at the very end of the
twelfth century to its final overthrow by the Moghuls in the
sixteenth century, is the story of a succession of invading
dynasties with origins beyond the North-West Frontier. In
the thirteenth century, the Mongols of Genghis Khan made
brief forays across this frontier to the banks of the Indus.
Tamerlane, in the early fifteenth century, staged a more impressive raid into the subcontinent which brought about the sack
of the great city of Delhi. There was a moment in the eighteenth
century when it looked as if a confederation of Afghan clans
would establish its rule over much of India's north; and in the
same century the Persian ruler, Nadir Shah, captured Delhi
and took off to Iran the Peacock Throne of the Moghul emperors who, themselves, had created an Indian empire following
invasion from the north-west two centuries before.

In the history of the subcontinent, the North-West Frontier
has played a role of an importance comparable with that of the
Great Wall frontier region of Chinese history. The sequence of

invasions goes far to explain many of the divisive and fragmentary aspects of Indian social and political evolution. The subcontinent usually managed to absorb its invaders, but it did so at a price: the inability to develop its political unification under the hammer blows of foreign attack. Some foreign invaders, moreover, were not easily absorbed. Islam came to the subcontinent across the North-West Frontier through a series of invasions beginning at the very end of the seventh century and culminating in the Muslim conquest of northern India in the thirteenth century. While the Hindu civilisation has without doubt influenced Islam in the subcontinent—it has, for example, infected it with some caste concepts—it was unable to prevent the region from evolving in modern times into two nations, basically Hindu India and Islamic Pakistan.

In its geopolitical structure, the North-West Frontier of the Indian subcontinent has from the earliest times been far more complex than that of the 'Inner Asian' frontier of China. The northern Chinese frontier divided a nomad world from a world of settled cultivators. The cultural and social institutions of the nomad were no match for the Chinese in a battle for survival on Chinese soil. Along the frontier of their sphere, the Chinese possessed the predominant civilising power. The Indian North-West Frontier, on the other hand, not only divided settled cultivators from nomads but also marked a line of separation between two major centres of civilisation, India and Iran. The nomads threatened both regions. The North-West Frontier of India was also the north-eastern frontier of Iran. The junction of these frontiers was a point of great weakness and the scene of conflict and competition. It was as if the line of the Great Wall of China were held by two states operating in an atmosphere of mutual antagonism. (See Map 8.)

From the point of view of the inhabitants of the Indian subcontinent—an outlook which the British tended to acquire along with their Indian empire—the invasions from the north-west looked like scourges of God for which no mortal explanation could be assigned. Suddenly, and without warning, the invaders would appear poised at the head of the Khyber or the Bolan pass, ready to rush down on the Indus plains like an avalanche on an Alpine village. In fact, of course, the presence of the invader was the product of political developments in

8. India and adjacent areas to the north-west.

Iran and Central Asia which might have had a long history before their impact was felt in the Indian plains. In this process we can detect a number of recurring themes.

One category of invasion had its origins in Iran. The Iranian plateau has possessed a history of unity which may well be compared with that of China. Through internal dynastic decay or the pressure of foreign invasion (usually from the north-east) the Iranian state has from time to time disintegrated; but the trend has always been towards reunification and Iranianisation of foreign regimes. When powerful, Iran has looked to the security of its eastern frontiers. It has attempted to check the nomad menace from the north-east, often adopting policies very similar to those which the Chinese traditionally applied in Central Asia. It has also sought to tidy up, as it were, the frontier zone comprising the regions today known as Afghanistan and Baluchistan. This process has on occasions carried Iranian power down to the Indus valley. For example, the Indus valley was part of the organisation into satrapies of the Achæmenian empire of Cyrus, Darius and Xerxes. When Alexander the Great conquered the Achæmenian state, it was inevitable that he should also acquire an interest in its eastern frontiers: a fact which goes far to explain his Indian adventure. The great Iranian dynasty of the Safavids in the sixteenth and seventeenth centuries was much interested in north-west India, which it considered much as did the Chinese consider such regions as Eastern Turkestan and Mongolia. In Safavid eyes, the Moghul emperors in Delhi were tributaries of the Shah-in-Shah.

Iranian history could affect India in quite another way. A powerful Iranian state could deflect the attention of kingdoms established in Afghanistan from the south-west to the south-east. Afghanistan was often the home of groups and dynasties which had failed on the great stage of world history provided by the Iranian plateau and the oases of Turkestan. The successors of Tamerlane, for example, excluded from Iran by the rising power of the Safavids and deprived of their Central Asian cities like Samarkand by the Uzbeks, still managed to maintain a foothold in the valleys of the Hindu Kush. From here they could only spread eastwards. The result was Babur's Indian campaigns which, in the early sixteenth century, laid the foundations of the Moghul empire.

The Indian plains were extremely vulnerable to adventurers from Afghanistan, like Mahmud of Ghazni and Babur. The cities of the subcontinent provided a rich field for plunder. The established Indian powers were unable to put up an effective united resistance to the nomad cavalry which constituted the core of such invading armies. On occasion (and we can find parallels for this in Chinese history as well), the invader was originally called in as a mercenary force by an Indian power, only to turn military aid into military conquest. Once established in the lowlands of the subcontinent, however, the invader found himself confronted with the same kind of threat which he had posed to his predecessors. Unless he could retain control of the Afghan highlands, he too would be subjected to attack from the north-west. He needed access to his old base, moreover, for it was here that he could recruit the cavalry forces upon which he relied for military supremacy. It was, however, always much easier to raid down into India from Afghanistan than to control Afghanistan from India. The very factors which made the invader's success possible in the first place also made him vulnerable to invasion by someone else. Here was the classic dilemma of the North-West Frontier. No lasting solution was found to it in pre-colonial times. The Moghuls, who built up what was certainly, at its height, the most powerful Indian state of pre-European times, were unable to create a lasting union between eastern Afghanistan and the Panjab. A major factor in Moghul decline in the seventeenth century was, without doubt, the resources expended in an attempt to hold the Afghan fortresses of Kabul and Kandahar.

Even the control by Delhi of Kabul and Kandahar would not have provided in itself a final solution to the problem of the North-West Frontier. The Kabul-Kandahar line—what in British times was to be known as the 'scientific frontier'—was threatened both from western Turkestan (by the Uzbeks, for example, in the Moghul period) and from Iran. To defend that line it was necessary to establish some influence over the course of political history to the north and to the west: to create, in other words, something which would perform the main functions of the Chinese 'protectorates' beyond the Wall.

The result of the nature of North-West Frontier history was to create a broad belt, stretching from the Pamirs and the Karakoram to the Persian Gulf and the Arabian Sea, in which no firm boundaries had ever been established, no equivalent of the line of the Chinese Wall. Here was a frontier zone involving both the hill country of Kashmir, Afghanistan and Baluchistan and the plains of the Indus, in which traditional boundaries did not exist. Had there been a traditional united Indian state, as there had for so long been a united Chinese state, then a boundary, protected by a system of external 'protectorates', might have emerged before the British set foot on the subcontinent. But no such tradition existed. The boundaries of the North-West Frontier today are a British creation, even though the problems involved in them may be of considerably greater antiquity.

3

The Rise of the
Imperial Frontier Systems

It has become fashionable to see the history of modern colonial expansion as being very much the product of Western greed. The former subjects of the European empires, even if impeccably capitalist in outlook, often detect a sinister design in the process which, during the nineteenth and early twentieth centuries, spread European power and influence across so much of the face of Asia and Africa. There is, of course, much truth in the thesis that the imperial powers acquired empires because they wanted empires; but to explain the entire process of empire-building in the light of some master plan or deliberate policy is seriously to oversimplify the issue. While no empire was entirely the outcome of accident, the result of a fit of absent-mindedness, the determination of the final limits of imperial expansion was often due to factors not entirely within the control of the imperial powers. Once embarked upon the extension of national influence beyond the metropolitan boundaries, it was often extremely difficult to call a halt to colonial acquisition.

The British Indian empire provides an admirable example of

this phenomenon. The British first came to the Indian sub-continent at the beginning of the seventeenth century as merchants. They did not seek territories; they wanted trade. For over a century, they managed to limit their Indian posses-sions to the minimum area which they felt was called for as a base for their commercial operations. It was not the policy of the East India Company, the authority under which the British Raj was created, to take over the Moghul empire. During the eighteenth century, however, the East India Company started to do just this. The collapse of Moghul power through internal discord and the pressure of the Mahrathas and the Afghans, combined with the possibility of a rising French influence detrimental to British interests, obliged the British to inter-vene actively in internal Indian politics. The result, in 1757, was the acquisition of Bengal: the crucial step which led by inevitable stages to the British conquest of the entire subcontinent.

Once in possession of one Indian province, the British were faced with the problem of the security of that province's frontier with districts not under their control. Frontier crises led to transfrontier campaigns and the extension of the fron-tier. The process continued until the sphere of British rule had reached what might be termed the natural frontier regions of the Southern Zone: the North-East Frontier and mainland South-east Asia, the Himalayan barrier and the hill tracts of the North-West Frontier. It was only at this stage that the British could begin the task of creating stable boundaries for their Indian territories; and it was not a process which had been completed by the time that Britain ceased to be an imperial power in the two decades immediately following the Second World War.

Like the British, the other two great European imperial powers on the Asian mainland, France and Russia, were also much influenced by these basic considerations of frontier policy.

E

The French, though they had competed with the British in India during the eighteenth century, and had at that time shown some interest in the trade and politics of mainland South-east Asia, did not lay the foundations for their Indo-chinese colonies until the middle of the nineteenth century. The French raid on Tourane (Da-nang) in 1858 and their capture of Saigon in the following year, were examples of imperialism at its worst. The French admirals who planned the Annamese adventure, however, could not have anticipated the full extent of the empire which they were creating. The Tourane and Saigon ventures, which were made jointly with the Spanish, were designed—so their public justification had it—to persuade the Vietnamese monarchy to stop persecuting Christian missionaries and to open the country to trade. The French re-inforced this argument with a resuscitation of the long defunct Franco-Annamese treaty of 1787: the so-called Treaty of Versailles which gave France the right to a commercial estab-lishment at Tourane in return for French aid for the Nguyen dynasty against its foes. Once started, however, the expansion of French power was not so easily checked. Control of Saigon inevitably led to control of the whole of Annam. It brought French rule into Cambodia and Tonkin, and, as a final stage in the 1890s, up the Mekong valley into Laos. To the north, expansion halted only when the borders of metropolitan China were reached. To the west and north-west, the French empire stopped growing when it reached a certain critical distance from the outposts of the British empire. The presence of the British in Burma prevented the French annexation of Siam and brought about the creation of a boundary between Laos and Burma along the Mekong river.

Similarly, the presence of the French in Indochina had a profound effect on British frontier policy. As the French moved westwards from Saigon, so the government of British India became increasingly concerned for the security of its own eastern flank in Burma. It should not be forgotten that, for

centuries of English history, the French had been the great
European foe. It was to a great extent in response to the French
challenge that Britain annexed Upper Burma in 1886, when
Lord Dufferin, the viceroy of India, reacted to the reports of
the establishment of French relations with the Mandalay kingdom by pushing forward the British frontier into the zone of
potential insecurity. British actions in Burma, in turn, accelerated the advance of French influence up the Mekong into Laos.
Tension increased as the British and French limits grew closer
to each other. There were contemporary observers who prophesied war between the two powers. Instead, however, there
began in the 1890s a series of Anglo-French discussions which
resulted in a definition of colonial boundaries. The precise
alignments of all the boundaries of mainland South-east Asia—
those of Burma, Thailand (Siam), Laos, Cambodia, the two
Vietnams and Malaya—derive directly or indirectly from these
discussions. (See Map 9.)

There are scholars who deny the importance of Anglo-French
competition as a major factor in imperial expansion in mainland
South-east Asia. For example, it has been argued that, while
Lord Dufferin justified to the government in London the
annexation of Upper Burma on the grounds that he was
obliged to counter French diplomacy at Mandalay, the real
reason for his action was to be found in the demands of the
British merchant community at Rangoon. In other words, the
French threat was used as a cloak to conceal purely commercial
interests. There can be no doubt that commercial interests did
indeed exist, but their significance can easily be exaggerated.
Another argument sometimes advanced is that British and
French frontier officers, obsessed with purely local administrative problems, exploited the French threat or the British threat,
to justify high-handed actions which their superiors would
otherwise have repudiated. Certainly, British officials like Sir
J. G. Scott and French officials like Auguste Pavie (the two
creators of the Franco-British boundary on the Mekong) did

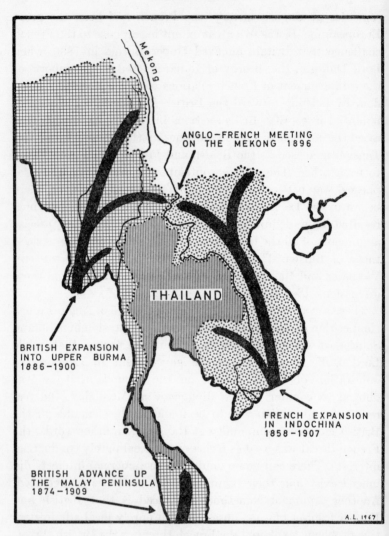

9. The Anglo-French frontier system in South-east Asia, with Thailand becoming a buffer between British and French territory.

act in this way. Yet they were able to do so only because Anglo-French competition was a fact and an established part of the political atmosphere in which they lived and worked.

The British and French empires in Asia were both founded and maintained by sea power. Nowhere were they in direct territorial contact with metropolitan France or the British Isles. They never became important areas for European settlement. The Russian empire was something quite different, since it could be described as the product of the eastwards expansion of the Russian state: a process analogous to the expansion of the Germans into the Slav lands of Eastern Europe. The Urals had nothing like the geopolitical significance of the English Channel or, even, of the Himalayan range. By the end of the sixteenth century, Russia, having reasserted itself after centuries of attack by Mongols and Turks of Central Asian origin, began to spread over the Urals. This was encouraged by the state, but the work of eastward expansion was very largely undertaken by what would today be called private enterprise. Traders and fur-trappers moved along the natural communications of the great Siberian rivers. Behind them came officials and missionaries: the agents of the Russian state and of Russian civilisation who watched over the process of settlement by Russian agricultura-lists. By the middle of the seventeenth century, Russia had extended its influence right across Siberia to the shores of the Pacific, thus outflanking the entire north of Chinese Central Asia. By the middle of the seventeenth century, the Russians had made their first tentative meeting with Chinese territorial power.

The initial stages of Russia's expansion to the east of the Urals took place in tracts which were but lightly populated by Ural-Altaic tribal groups who could not present serious opposition to the Russian advance. Both the pace and the direction of the Russian march to the Pacific were dictated more by the nature of the natural highways of the Siberian river system than by official policy. In many ways, the eastward advance of the Russian frontier in Siberia resembled the westward progress of the European frontier in North America. The territories occupied by settlers were integrated into an expanding state; they did not become the nuclei of new sovereignties. Expansion and absorption continued until a natural limit was reached; in the case of both Russia and America, this was the Pacific Ocean.

The Siberian communications by river and portage rapidly brought the Russians to the Pacific and to the northern edge of the Chinese sphere along the Mongolian and Manchurian frontiers in the region of Lake Baikal and the southern watersheds of the basin of the river Lena. The great Siberian rivers, however, by-passed the Islamic Central Asian khanates of Bokhara, Khiva and Kokand, which controlled the oasis cities of western Turkestan. In this tract of desert and mountain to the east of the Caspian there had been a measure of Russian diplomatic and commercial penetration during the eighteenth century, but Russian political domination here was not to be accomplished until the nineteenth century. It took place in two distinct stages. First: between about 1800 and 1855, the line of fortified posts along the Siberian frontier was pushed southwards until it reached the Aral Sea and Lake Balkhash. The result was Russian control over steppe and semi-desert which, during the eighteenth century, had been the scene of active competition between nomadic Kazakh tribal confederations (hordes). Second: between 1855 and the end of the century, the Russians advanced across desert and mountain tracts to occupy the oasis cities of the Central Asian khanates concentrated in the basins of the Oxus (Amu Darya) and Jaxartes (Syr Darya) rivers, which flow northwards from the Pamirs and the Tien Shan ranges into the Aral Sea.

Western Turkestan and the Central Asian khanates could, in pre-European times, be classified as falling within the Iranian sphere. Here was the north-eastern frontier zone of the Iranian state, and in periods of Iranian political decline invasion and conquest had come from this direction. The Timurids, for example, in the fourteenth century conquered Iran from their base at Samarkand in Turkestan. In periods of Iranian dynastic strength, it was inevitable that thought should be given to the protection of this frontier; thus, the Safavids sought in the sixteenth century to neutralise the power in Turkestan of the Uzbeks. Russian penetration into this Iranian frontier region, therefore, seemed to imply as great a threat to Iran proper as had Russian advances into the north-western fringes of Iran from the Caucasus in the early nineteenth century. By threatening Iran, the Russians were also threatening the western flank of British India. Just as French expansion towards the eastern frontiers of the Indian subcontinent produced British counter-measures, so Russian pressure on the Iranian world provoked a response from British India. As Burma was to Siam and Indochina, so the Indus valley, Baluchistan and Afghanistan were to Iran and Turkestan.

In detail, the histories of these two frontier zones on the flanks of the Indian subcontinent were very different. There were problems in the north-western area which were not to be found in the north-eastern. It was not possible in practice to deal with Iran and Afghanistan as Siam and Burma were dealt with by the colonial powers. Even so, the principles of colonial boundary evolution which were applied in these two regions were basically similar. As the colonial empires approached each other, there developed a period of tension between them—accompanied by prophesies of war—which was followed by a period of negotiation and boundary settlement.

The stages of colonial advance—the reaction to local circumstances and the struggle to find a satisfactory colonial limit—were often involuntary. In 1864, the Russian foreign minister, Prince Gortchakoff, gave a theoretical explanation of one facet of this question when he explained in a circular to the major European powers why the Russians were expanding their rule into Turkestan. The Russians, Gortchakoff declared, had no

wish to go on annexing khanate after khanate. All they wanted
was a peaceful frontier. However, when faced with turbulence
beyond their frontier of the moment, they had no option but to
undertake a further advance. The mechanism of which Gortchakoff gave one expression was virtually impossible to check
until the potential areas of transfrontier turbulence had all been
brought under some kind of imperial control.

By the end of the nineteenth century, the major problem of
imperial frontier policy in Asia concerned the meeting points of
the three great empires of Russia, Britain and France. The
result was the creation of an elaborate boundary system separating the three colonial spheres. Work continued on the system
right up to the Second World War; in this the Soviet Russians
followed in the footsteps of their tsarist predecessors. However,
the great period of imperial frontier evolution came to an end
with the outbreak of the First World War. During the early
years of the twentieth century, frontier policy was much
influenced by the fact that the three main imperial powers
were becoming allied to each other in the context of European
diplomacy. The need to meet the growing challenge of Germany
facilitated Asian settlement and the resultant concessions.

The major principle behind the Asian frontier system was
recognition of the desirability of avoiding direct contact
between the administered territories of the various colonial
empires concerned. If possible there should be no common
boundary between empires, rather there should be interposed a
buffer territory. The nature of the buffer varied very much
according to circumstances. Iran, Afghanistan, Chinese Turkestan, Tibet, Mongolia, Siam—even China proper—all became
buffer regions during the late nineteenth and early twentieth
centuries, even if in some cases rather subtle and indirect ones.
The term 'buffer' describes accurately enough the function of
these regions. They served as an elastic substance placed
between the unyielding fabric of colonial sovereignties. They
could bend and bounce in a way that the defined boundaries of

colonies could not. They prevented the clash of colonial interests from leading to conflicts which would prove extremely difficult to control once metropolitan public opinion was aroused.

In some cases, the creation of buffers involved boundary delimitation or demarcation. The buffer system between the

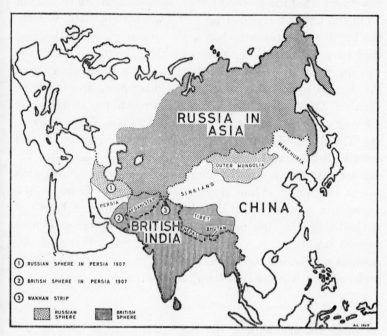

10. The Anglo-Russian frontier system in Asia as it had evolved by 1914. Note how the Wakhan strip of Afghanistan prevents British and Russian territory from actually touching.

Russian and British empires produced the boundaries of the North-West Frontier zone. (See Map 10.) Between 1869 and 1896, there emerged a delimited, and in some cases demarcated, boundary between Russia and Iran and Afghanistan which stretched from the Caspian to the Pamirs. At the same time, the British evolved a defined boundary between their territory and

Iran and Afghanistan—much of it by means of the Anglo-Afghan agreement of 1893 which set out verbally the so-called Durand Line. This process established the physical limits of the buffer. Its political nature was then defined by direct Anglo-Russian negotiation. The Anglo-Russian Convention of 1907 set out clearly what the British and the Russians could and could not do in the buffer tracts of Iran and Afghanistan. Here, because the buffer territories marched with both empires and because they were sovereignties in their own right, boundary definition was an essential prerequisite for political settlement. Part of the Afghan buffer, the narrow strip of territory known as the Wakhan Tract where the Hindu Kush meets the Pamirs, was the result of what can only be described as boundary engineering. The Afghans were reluctant to accept sovereignty for this remote district, and only did so under imperial pressure. We can see a similar process of boundary engineering in operation to the north-east of the British Indian empire where, in the 1890s, a meeting between British Burma and French Laos was devised along the Mekong. This particular line accorded with no ancient traditions; it was the product of Anglo-French diplomacy as a substitute for a neutral buffer which would have been preferred but which it was found impracticable to create.

*

At their greatest extent, the three European powers on the Asian mainland—Russia, Britain and France—possessed a far longer frontier with Chinese-influenced, protected or administered territory than they did with any other region. It was inevitable, therefore, that China should play a crucial part in the evolution of the imperial frontier systems. The powers adopted three main approaches to the Chinese problem. First: China could be regarded as being in some respects an imperial power in its own right. Second: portions of the Chinese sphere could at times appear to be useful raw material for the creation of buffer tracts analogous to Iran, Afghanistan or Siam. Third:

there existed arguments for the extension of the colonial empires far beyond the limits of the traditional Chinese frontier —in other words, for the imperial annexation of metropolitan Chinese territory. These three views of the Chinese role were often conflicting in their implications, and it is not easy to fit the history of the relations between China and the imperial powers into the framework of a single pattern. We must confine ourselves here to a few examples.

Throughout their period of imperial power in Asia, the British tended to be anxious lest their diplomacy towards both China and states considered as falling within the Chinese sphere might produce an adverse effect on the British commercial position in China. In 1814–16, for example, when Britain was at war with Nepal (a country thought to be in some way tributary to the Chinese emperor), the Indian government endeavoured to minimise the risk of Chinese reprisals against the East India Company's trade at Canton, the main source of its profits at that time. With this consideration in mind, the British did not annex Nepal at the end of the war, preferring to keep it intact as a kind of buffer between their territory and what they regarded as the Chinese imperial outposts in Tibet. A similar outlook, in the middle of the nineteenth century, governed British relations with the Himalayan states of Sikkim and Bhutan. In their dealings with Tibet in the period 1886–1914, despite strong temptations to the contrary, the British never thought it expedient entirely to ignore Chinese interests in Lhasa. Had China been throughout the nineteenth century the power it was to become in the 1950s following the establishment of the Chinese People's Republic, there can be little doubt that the British would have established a buffer tract along the entire Himalayan range between Kashmir and the Assam-Burma border. Had this happened there would, perhaps, have been no Kashmir dispute between India and Pakistan and no Sino-Indian conflict in the Himalayas.

In the second half of the nineteenth century, it seemed to

many European observers that Central Asia was about to slip away from the sphere of Chinese influence. In these circumstances, regions like Tibet, Chinese Turkestan (Sinkiang) and Mongolia tended to appear as potential buffer tracts for the British and Russian imperial possessions along the flanks of which they were situated. Chinese Turkestan was an obvious extension of the Iranian and Afghan buffers between British and Russian territory. Mongolia for Russia and Tibet for Britain held rather more subtle buffer properties since each was in direct contact with but one European power; but there were none the less attractive arguments in support of the extension of European influence into these frontier tracts of the Chinese empire in a period of growing Chinese political and military weakness.

Chinese weakness, of course, could lead to more than the extension of European influence; it might result in major imperial annexations. There were clear signs by the end of the nineteenth century that Russia hoped to extend its Pacific border south of the Amur into Manchuria. Russia was to be frustrated, however, by the Japanese: the first Asians to experiment successfully with the modern European brand of imperialism. The French saw Yunnan as a logical direction in which to continue their colonial expansion from Tonkin, and their acquisition of the port of Kwangchowan in 1899 (returned to China in 1945) could well be interpreted as the first step in a French advance along the Kwangtung coast towards the British colonial possessions on the mainland opposite Hong Kong. In British eyes, at least, from the 1870s there existed the possibility that the Russians would annex Chinese Turkestan as they had annexed the Central Asian khanates.

The Chinese suffered greatly from the process of imperial expansion during the nineteenth and early twentieth centuries, but less so than a contemporary observer might at times have prophesied. After the advance to the Amur in the 1850s, which was but a repetition of what the Russians had tried to do in the seventeenth century, the tsarist government acquired far less Chinese territory than might have been expected. Japanese pressure prevented the Russians from taking over Manchuria and Korea during the period of the Boxer troubles and their immediate aftermath. Most of the Ili territory in Sinkiang which the Russians occupied in 1871 (on the grounds that they needed to maintain law and order across their border) was returned to China in 1881. In the 1890s, Russia dispossessed the Chinese of their rather nominal rights in the Pamirs. At the time of the Chinese Revolution of 1911, the Russians obtained a very powerful influence in an autonomous Outer Mongolia, but in name the region remained Chinese and it has to this day avoided outright Russian annexation. At the same period, Russia became the dominant force in much of Sinkiang, though the continuity of Chinese administration there was never shattered. During this period, moreover, the French were not able to take Yunnan under their wing, as some senior officials of the Indochinese government hoped; and the British did not create a protectorate over Tibet, where the Chinese managed to cling to a kind of residual sovereignty which they could exploit at some subsequent moment of strength.

Behind these successes on the periphery of their state lay the greatest Chinese success of all: the avoidance of total partition between the powers and the disappearance of even the nucleus of a sovereign government. To some degree, this achievement must be credited to the abilities—often neglected in European and American writing—of the statesmen and diplomatists in the service of the Manchu dynasty. Manchu China evinced a great deal of ineptitude, but it also mustered real skill and determination when the national need called for it. Even so, it is unlikely that any Chinese official, however able, could have met the challenge of colonial pressure had it been presented as a single and united force. Fortunately for China, the colonial powers were in active competition with each other even when ostensibly in alliance. By 1907, the four major powers in territorial contact with China—Britain, Russia, France and Japan, the only Asian member and newly elected to the club— were all so tied to each other by a complex of treaties that no one power could move without giving the other compensation else- where. In theory, a situation of this kind could have resulted in the total dismemberment of China. In practice, it had the oppo- site effect. France, for example, could not advance in Yunnan without a British co-operation that was not forthcoming. The British could not extend their influence into Tibet without offering Russia advantages elsewhere which they were ex- tremely reluctant to do. The alliances among the four powers were perhaps most effective in preventing outsiders (Germany, for instance) from taking effective steps towards the creation of an empire on Chinese soil. Thus, in a very real sense, the process which subjected China to 'unequal treaties' and which modern Chinese statesmen constantly denounce, also helped to ensure the survival of an independent Chinese state. The greatest threat to Chinese sovereignty in modern times was to come, not from the imperial powers acting in concert, but from a single power, Japan, embarking upon a policy of Chinese conquest in defiance of world opinion; and, even in this circumstance, involvement by other powers was without doubt a major factor in China's survival.

By the time of the Chinese Revolution of 1911, the imperial frontier system of Britain, Russia and France, with the growing Japanese sphere added to it, completely enclosed the Chinese world. This, in the long run, was the greatest significance of the frontier system. For the Chinese, it transformed the nature of the traditional frontier problem as it has been outlined in an earlier chapter. The 'Inner Asian' frontier line was now threat- ened by forces other than those of nomad kingdoms; it was under pressure from the Russians and, to a lesser degree, from the British. There was a finite possibility that the European imperial frontiers might reach the line of the Great Wall. It was no longer enough for the Chinese to maintain their influence in

Central Asia by indirect rule and a system of 'protectorates'. They had, if they were to guarantee their control of the frontier, to bring it under direct Chinese administration. Such a policy was initiated in Chinese Turkestan in the 1870s, where the Chinese defeat of Yakub Beg was followed by the creation of what amounted to a new Chinese province, Sinkiang. In about 1900, a similar policy was developed towards Mongolia and Tibet. In Mongolia, the Chinese failed, and Outer Mongolia is now an independent state free of Chinese sovereignty. In Tibet, however, the Chinese were more successful. Today, Tibet is the 'Tibet Region of the Chinese People's Republic'.

In the traditional Chinese frontier situation, the south-west was a direction in which the Chinese were expanding slowly but from which they anticipated no major threat to their security. With the creation of the Anglo-French frontier stretching from the edge of Tibet to the Gulf of Tonkin, no intelligent Chinese statesman could escape the conclusion that Yunnan was indeed threatened. The Chinese showed themselves to be unexpectedly active on this frontier. They resisted the French occupation of Tonkin and opposed British exploring missions from Burma. Their diplomatists fought hard and long to keep the boundary line between Yunnan and British Burma as far to the west as possible. The Chinese opposition to a boundary along the Salween-Irrawaddy watershed was not as unreasonable and as provocative as the British tended to think.

Chinese statesmen had always been aware of the frontier. The dynastic histories made it clear that an active frontier policy was the corollary of a strong and undivided Chinese state. Never before, however, had the Chinese faced a frontier threat so constant and so extensive as that created by the building of the Russian, British and French frontier systems in Asia during the nineteenth and early twentieth centuries. To the European threat, by the end of the nineteenth century, was added the menace of the Japanese which was to bring about, not only a partition of China, but also a collapse of the European imperial defences in mainland South-east Asia. The lessons of this era have not been forgotten, and there can be no doubt that they influence profoundly the modern Chinese attitude to frontier questions.

A great deal of the boundary between China and the European empires in Asia was not only created but also delimited or demarcated in the colonial era. The greater part of the Russo-Sinkiang boundary was laid down in the 1880s, and the Russo-Manchurian boundary in the Amur region was defined in 1858–60. The boundary between French Indochina and China was determined in the last two decades of the nineteenth century, and no serious doubt exists today as to its alignment. In general, the boundary between British Burma and Yunnan had been defined by 1941—the final sectors through League of Nations arbitration in the 1930s.* While the Chinese have not always been prepared to accept the legitimacy of all these proceedings which resulted in boundary definitions, they have on the whole refrained in recent years from offering a serious physical challenge to boundary alignments of this kind which they have inherited from previous regimes.

One major boundary line which was not so well defined in the great days of the imperial frontier systems was that running through the long mountain frontier tract between British India and Chinese Central Asia. Here, largely because of the conflicting roles which China played in the game of British imperial strategy—as a power to be wooed, as a potential zone of buffer states and as a possible field for colonial expansion—much of the frontier zone was not traversed by clearly demarcated boundary alignments. From the Pamirs to the Nepalese

* On behalf of the League of Nations, the Iselin Commission examined on the ground the Sino-Burmese border in the region of the Wa states. Most of its proposals were accepted in principle by Anglo-Chinese agreement in 1941. The Kuomintang government then had second thoughts, but the Sino-Burmese Boundary Agreement of 1960 appears to have followed the broad lines of the Iselin Commission award.

border in the Himalayas, no firm border line had been settled, though a number of possibilities had been given theoretical consideration by the British. The sovereignty of an area of 20,000 square miles or so remained in doubt, at least in the minds of some officials in Whitehall and Simla. Farther east, a short stretch of boundary between Sikkim and Tibet had been delimited in the Anglo-Chinese Convention of 1890, though efforts to secure joint demarcation with the Tibetans had failed. Farther east again, between Bhutan and Burma, lay the Assam Himalayan hill tracts where Anglo-Tibetan agreement in 1914 had produced the delimited McMahon Line boundary; but the Chinese had good grounds for contesting the validity of the treaty basis of this line, and in recent times they have done so. The result has been a Chinese claim to more than 30,000 square miles of territory at present administered by India as part of the North-East Frontier Agency (NEFA).

★

Whether well enough defined (as in the case of the border between French Indochina and China) or for much of its length undefined (as in the case of the Sino-Indian border in British times), the imperial frontier system was in the last resort maintained by imperial power. In the middle decades of the twentieth century, in great measure as a consequence of the impact of the Second World War on the political and economic strength of Europe, the British and French empires in Asia suddenly came to an end. By late 1954, the French had withdrawn from Indochina and had handed over to the government in New Delhi their enclaves along the coast of the Indian subcontinent.*

* French India consisted of five enclaves: Mahé (on the Malabar coast), Karikal, Pondicherry and Yanaon (on the Coromandel coast), and Chandernagore (on the Hughli river above Calcutta). Pondicherry, the largest of the enclaves, was the capital of French India.

Unlike the French, the Portuguese endeavoured to cling on to the remnants of their empire. Goa, the last Portuguese possession in the

F

In 1947, after a presence of more than three centuries, the
British left India. By 1966, they retained on the Asian mainland
only the colony of Hong Kong and a group of protectorates in
the Arabian peninsula along the Gulf of Aden, the Arabian Sea
and the Persian Gulf. The surrender of colonial territory was
accompanied by a disappearance of colonial influence in transfrontier buffer tracts. Britain ceased to be a major factor in the
internal politics of Iran, Afghanistan, Nepal and Tibet. By the
end of the Second World War, France had been obliged to give
up its ambition to create a special sphere of interest in Yunnan,
and had returned to China its settlement on the Kwangtung
coast, Kwangchowan. By 1960, the views of London or Paris
had ceased to be of paramount concern to the Thai authorities
in Bangkok.

All this happened in the Southern Zone. It was not accompanied by a corresponding decentralisation of power in the
Russian or Chinese Zones. The Soviet Union adhered with
determination to the tsarist conquests in Central Asia. China,
following the communist victory in 1950, soon established a
power along its land borders such as it had never possessed
before. In contrast to the proliferation of new states in the
Southern Zone, the Russian and Chinese Zones in the twentieth
century have seen the emergence or revival of only three mainland sovereignties apart from Russia and China. Outer Mongolia evolved from a Chinese frontier protectorate into a fully
independent state, at least in international law, and probably at
this moment in fact as well. Korea, after a history of Chinese
protection followed by Japanese control, has been partitioned
into two sovereignties quite as distinct as those obtaining in the
two Vietnams. Much of the old tsarist frontier system, however,

subcontinent, was invaded and annexed by India in 1961. Already by
the eighteenth century the Portuguese empire in Asia was of but the
slightest geopolitical significance. The Portuguese still retain Macao on
the Chinese mainland near Hong Kong, but it is clear that they do
so only because it is not in the Chinese interest to expel them.

has survived into modern times. The distinction between the colonial and post-colonial eras, so clear in the Southern Zone, is rather blurred in the Russian and Chinese Zones where the change has been in regime and political philosophy rather than in the nature of territorial sovereignty. It is in the Southern Zone, therefore, that we will find the widest selection of examples of the legacy of imperial frontiers and boundaries for the rulers of modern Asia.

The boundaries of the newly independent states of Asia are the boundaries which were inherited from the colonial regimes to which they have succeeded. These boundaries—the product of the evolution of the imperial frontier systems, and based on the strategic, political and economic necessities of colonial policy—now have to serve as the cell walls of national identities. In some cases they do this well enough; in others they do not. The rulers of newly independent states cannot be blamed for unsatisfactory boundaries which were not of their making; but they have, none the less, to deal with the problems that such boundaries pose. In doing so, however, they rarely enjoy the freedom of action which their imperial predecessors possessed.

With independence, what was once the distant possession of a colonial power became transformed into the motherland or fatherland of a sovereign nationality. What was the basis of that sovereignty and that sense of national identity? The colonial statesman at the moment of the transfer of power might answer thus: 'We bequeath to you sovereignty over the colony of such-and-such, and what you have is what we hand over to you.' In other words, independent India is British India (minus, of course, Pakistan), and it is independent India because it *was* British India. The process, in this view, can be compared with the transfer of a freehold. Ownership changes, but the property is the same. There is much legal force here, but it is not matched by a corresponding emotional force. The Indian nationalist would say that, with the transfer of power, India had won its freedom. The clear implication is that an independent India had existed before the colonial period and was now being resurrected. The colonial era was not the basis of national sovereignty; it was but an intermission in the story of national development. An analogy, perhaps, can be found in the return of France to a sovereign French government after the period of German occupation.

There were, of course, national identities in Asia in the pre-colonial era. Some Asian states, like Iran and Thailand, managed to survive into modern times without having to go through a period of direct colonial rule, though all Asian states had to accept colonial influence and supervision. No Asian state came through the colonial period with its boundaries unmodified. Through the operation of imperial policy, some acquired large tracts of territory which they could not possibly have secured or retained on their own; others lost, or consider that they have lost, extensive portions of their patrimony because of the action of colonial powers. All, to a greater or lesser extent, owe the present alignment of their boundaries to historical processes which took place during the colonial era.

The colonial factor in Asian boundary evolution, unpalatable though it may be to the sentiments of Asian nationalism, cannot be ignored. The settlement of disputed boundaries in the post-colonial age can be achieved only on the basis of an accurate determination of the whereabouts and nature of such boundaries in the colonial period. There has been a temptation to try to go back beyond the colonial precedent and to base national limits on 'traditional' criteria. In practice, however, such criteria have been extremely difficult to establish without much historical falsification. In the first place, the very concept of a modern defined boundary has not always been present in the political thought of Asia before the imposition of European influence. Thus, it is quite possible that some Asian states, even though of respectable antiquity, did not have in earlier times anything which could now be described as a proper boundary at all. In such circumstances, the quest for ancient and 'traditional' border alignments could well be fruitless. In the second place, the accurate definition of boundaries, even when they have had a long history, has depended upon the techniques of surveying and cartography which Europe brought to Asia. In many cases, whatever the merits or historical arguments, adequate documentation for pre-colonial boundaries simply does not exist. On both these counts, the system of colonial boundaries, even if accepted with extreme reluctance, is a major part of the legacy of the colonial empires in Asia to their successors.

PART II

Legacies of the Imperial Age

4

The North-West Frontier: Iran and Afghanistan

To the British, just as much as to their Moghul predecessors, the North-West Frontier of the Indian subcontinent posed a major problem of defence. For the Moghuls, the threat came from indigenous Asian powers like the Persians, the Afghans and the Uzbeks of Turkestan; for the British, the major menace appeared to arise from the policy of another European power, tsarist Russia, established on the Asian continent. The Russian factor conditioned the nature of British relations with the states to the north-west of the Indian empire. From the beginning of the nineteenth century right up to the end of the British Raj in 1947, Iran and Afghanistan were seen by British strategists as the potential gateways for the expansion of Russian influence, be it military or political, into the Indian plains where a handful of British soldiers and administrators controlled a subject population numbering hundreds of millions of souls. To a considerable degree, moreover, these fears were reciprocated in Russian minds. British policy along the frontier tracts of north-western India was interpreted by many Russian officers as being directed towards the undermining of Russian control over the oases of western Turkestan. In a real sense, the celebrated North-West Frontier was also the south-east frontier of imperial Russia: a zone where the policies of the two empires interacted, sometimes in conflict and sometimes in concert, with the most profound consequences for the evolution of boundaries of the modern states of Iran and Afghanistan.

IRAN

During the course of the nineteenth century, the Russians penetrated into the Iranian sphere from the Caucasus and from the deserts of Transcaspia. During the same period, the British despatched military expeditions from their bases in the Indus plains on to the Afghan highlands along the eastern side of the Hindu Kush. However, while profoundly influenced by colonial politics, neither Iran nor Afghanistan came under permanent Russian or British imperial rule. Instead, the two regions were turned into a system of buffer tracts between the centres of Russian and British power: a process which received formal acknowledgement in the Anglo-Russian Convention of 1907. Iran was divided into three zones, one adjacent to Russian territory and under predominant Russian influence, one adjacent to British India and under predominant British influence, and the third a neutral tract in between—a buffer within a buffer. Afghanistan, by the same agreement, was defined as being generally within the British sphere of influence, but in such a way as to appear to offer no challenge to the stability of Russia's control over its Central Asian possessions. The 1907 Convention was agreed to in an atmosphere of Anglo-Russian rapprochement, but its successful negotiation was possible only because it marked the culmination of a long process of boundary definition between both British and Russian territory and Iran and Afghanistan: a process which was more often the product of Anglo-Russian rivalry than Anglo-Russian collaboration. Boundaries once defined have remained. The Anglo-Russian Convention of 1907 is now long

dead and buried in the graveyard of obsolete treaties; the
system of boundaries upon which it is based, however,
survives to this day as a vital part of the imperial legacy
to the governments now ruling in Teheran and Kabul. (See
Map 11.)

11. Iran.

When the Russians, in the 1850s, began their southwards
advance from the Kazakhstan steppes into the basin of the
Oxus and Jaxartes rivers, where flourished the khanates of
Khiva, Kokand and Bukhara, they were moving into territory
which had possessed a long historical relationship with Iran
and had, in earlier periods, been under the control of dynasties

also ruling in Iran proper. At least since Safavid times, however, the Iranian central government had looked on the Central Asian tracts to the north and north-east of its province of Khorasan as being a source of danger rather than a desirable prize of conquest or possession. The Turkmen nomads of what is now Russian Turkmenistan were continually raiding Iranian soil, devastating the border tracts and, on occasions, penetrating across the central Iranian desert to Isfahan and Fars. In the early seventeenth century, Shah Abbas, the great Safavid ruler, began a policy of settling Kurdish, Turkish and Baluchi soldiers along this frontier to create there a permanent and self-reproducing defensive force, rather like the imperial Roman *limes*; and this policy was continued into the nineteenth century. In these circumstances, the Russian conquest of the Turkmen territory north of Khorasan came eventually to be seen in Iran less as a territorial loss than as a long-awaited final solution to the nomad threat.

By treaty in 1869, the mouth of the Atrak river was affirmed as the western (Caspian) end of the Russo-Khorasan boundary. In 1881, following the Russian campaign against the Tekke Turkmen, the middle sector of this boundary—from the Atrak river (flowing into the Caspian) to Sarakhs on the Hari Rud with its sources in Afghanistan—was delimited; shortly afterwards, in 1884–86, it was demarcated by a Russo-Persian boundary commission. The extreme eastern sector—following the Hari Rud south from Sarakhs to Zulfikar on the Afghan border—was delimited in 1893 and demarcated in 1894–95. On the eve of the First World War, there was a period when it looked as if tsarist policy was directed towards a southward deflection of this line to embrace Khorasan with its capital at Meshed; but the danger was averted.* In 1919, following the outbreak of the Russian Revolution, the Persians endeavoured

---

* The danger could be said to have arisen once more in 1941–46, when Khorasan formed part of the Soviet Zone in Iran; but again the Russians in the end withdrew to the 1881 line.

to establish a claim to the north of the 1881 line which would give them Merv (Mary) and some of the Tekke Turkmen territory. They were not successful. In 1921, the Persians signed an agreement with the Soviet government in which the 1881 line was confirmed, and since then Russo-Persian discussions over this section of border have been confined to matters relating to frontier crossing and water use.

The creation of the present Russo-Persian border from the Caspian to the Hari Rud marked the end of what had hitherto been a fundamental process in Iranian history: the invasions of Persian settled territory by Central Asian nomad bands. The Russians did what no Iranian dynasty had managed to do: they established an effective control over nomad activity in Turkestan. Iran no longer had to fear major attack from the north-east by Turkmen tribes, and with this route of external reinforcement closed, in modern times the Iranian government of the Pahlavi dynasty has been able to solve the problem of nomad groups living within the Iranian borders.

The British advance to the western edge of the Indus valley, like the Russian advance into Turkmen territory, brought about European political contact with a tribal zone on the Iranian frontier. Baluchistan, desolate though much of it is, has throughout recorded history provided one of the channels of communication between the Iranian plateau and the Indian subcontinent. On returning from his Indian adventure, Alexander the Great marched with his army along the Makran coast of Baluchistan. Arab armies followed this route in the opposite direction, from Iran to Sind, at the turn of the seventh and eighth centuries of our era. The tribal chiefs of Baluchistan, be they Baluchi (of Aryan stock) or Brahui (believed to be related to the Dravidians of south India), acquired during the course of their turbulent history fluctuating relationships with Iran, India and the ruling Afghan clans. The importance of Quetta, the strategic gateway to Kandahar in south-east Afghanistan, made it inevitable that the British should include the bulk of the Baluchistan tribal area within their Indian empire. During the 1860s and 1870s, with some further modification in 1905, the boundary between British Baluchistan and Iran was in general outline defined. The result was by no means a perfect ethnic or economic divide, since there remained closely related Baluchi tribal groups on both sides of the line, and in the central sector of the Iran-Baluchistan border there existed unresolved disputes over the waters of the Mashkel stream. Minor problems along this frontier, however, caused the British very little concern; their main interest in the boundaries of Baluchistan related to Afghanistan. The precise alignment of the Iran-Baluchistan border, moreover, became a matter of purely academic interest to the Indian government when, by the Anglo-Russian Convention of 1907, it was confirmed in possession of a sphere of influence in Seistan and Persian Baluchistan on the Iranian side.

There were to be periods between 1900 and 1947, and particularly during the two world wars, when the British virtually took over the administration of Iranian tracts to the west of the Baluchistan border, and when the Iranian town of Zahedan—the terminus of the railway from Quetta—became to all intents and purposes an outpost of the British Raj. Had such circumstances arisen in an earlier period, they would probably have resulted in annexation and a westward advance of the boundary at the expense of Iran. In the event, however, the transfer of power in 1947 was not accompanied by a Pakistani domination of Seistan and Persian Baluchistan. In fact, after 1947, for a while there existed a power vacuum along the Iranian side of the Pakistani border which gave rise to some friction and which focused attention on British omissions in boundary definition in this region. The late 1950s saw Iranian-Pakistani negotiations which, in 1960, resulted in a boundary treaty. Pakistan transferred to Iran a small tract (about 300 square miles in area) in exchange for which Iran renounced all claims to the remainder of the former British possessions in Baluchistan and accepted the old British boundary thus modified.*

The imperial frontier system also embraced the boundary between Iran and Afghanistan. In a very real sense, Afghanistan —and particularly its western part—is an extension of the Iranian sphere. Persian is still a major Afghan language. Herat, the largest city of western Afghanistan, is in many ways a Persian city and had been under Persian rule during the great days of the Safavid dynasty in the sixteenth and early seventeenth centuries. In the mid-eighteenth century, the Afghan forces of Ahmad Shah Abdali acquired Herat during the period of Iranian decline which followed the murder of Nadir Shah in 1747. In the 1830s, and again in the 1850s, the Persians endeavoured to recapture Herat. Their ambition, encouraged by Russia, was actively discouraged by Britain, which went to war with Persia over the Herat issue in 1856. British strategists saw the city as commanding one of the key routes from the west towards the passes of the Hindu Kush leading to the Indus plains. By the Anglo-Persian peace treaty of 1857, Herat was recognised as being within Afghanistan, and the Perso-Afghan frontier was defined sufficiently clearly to preclude future disputes of major significance, at least so long as the British remained as arbitrators. In recent years, this boundary has been stable enough, and will be increasingly so as the economic and political development of Afghanistan proceeds. Here the Persians lost under imperial pressure what they regarded as

* There were people in Pakistan who resented the Pakistani-Iranian boundary agreement and denied that the Pakistani government possessed the constitutional right to transfer territory to an alien power. The agreement was contested in the High Court of Pakistan, and contested with all the greater vehemence because of the widespread belief in Pakistan that it involved the cession of 3,000 square miles, rather than 300 square miles, as was the case. The episode illustrates clearly the new attitude towards frontier tracts in Asia. In the British period, the settlement of a boundary as remote as this would probably not have come to public notice at all.

part of their territory. They gained, however, in securing a
relatively trouble-free eastern flank: an enormous saving in
military and financial resources.

AFGHANISTAN

Afghanistan is a land-locked state with the mountains of the
Hindu Kush as its nucleus. It is entirely surrounded by boundaries created as a result of British and Russian imperial
frontier policy. The process of boundary-making gave to the
ruling Afghan dynasty during the nineteenth century control
over territory and populations which, in other circumstances, it
might never have acquired. British aid, both military and
diplomatic, enabled the Afghans to retain Herat in the face of
Persian attack. The devising of the Anglo-Russian frontier
system gave them a boundary along the Oxus river, thus putting under the rule of Kabul districts between the Oxus and
the Hindu Kush watershed which had up to that time also
possessed other allegiances. (See Map 12.)

Unaided, it is extremely unlikely that the Kabul authorities would have been able to dominate northern districts like
Maimana or Badakshan; these would most probably have
gravitated towards the Russian sphere had it not been for the
need to create an Anglo-Russian buffer. Discussion in Europe
between Britain and Russia in the period 1869–73 had established the principle of the Oxus boundary for Afghanistan.
Following the Panjdeh crisis of 1885, when the Russians seemed
about to advance up the Murghab river to the crests of the
Hindu Kush, the Oxus line was linked westwards with the
northern boundary of Iran by the work of an Anglo-Russian
boundary commission. Following the Pamirs crisis of the early
1890s, when the Russians approached dangerously close to the
northern frontier of Kashmir, the Oxus line was extended eastwards to meet Chinese Turkestan in the Pamirs, thereby creating the narrow Wakhan strip separating Russian from British
territory. This, again, was the work of an Anglo-Russian

commission (though with rather nominal Afghan participation) which laid down the boundary on the ground in 1895. The devising of the Wakhan buffer—a typical piece of imperial boundary engineering—produced as an incidental by-product a short stretch of border between Afghan and Chinese territory, perhaps less than fifty miles in all. Ignored during the British

12. Afghanistan. A-B: Boundary settled by Anglo-Russian Boundary Commission, 1886–87. B-C: Oxus boundary evolved in principle by Anglo-Russian diplomacy, 1869–73. C-D: Pamirs boundary defined by Anglo-Russian Boundary Commission, 1895. E-F: Durand Line, 1893 (1) Sino-Afghan border defined by treaty, 1963; (2) Bajaur district, where the Durand Line was still undefined in 1947.

G

period, it was delimited by Sino-Afghan treaty in 1963 and demarcated in the following year.

As to the north of the crests of the Hindu Kush, so also in the south along the edge of the Registan desert and the swamps of the lower Helmand in Zabulistan, Afghanistan during the colonial era was confirmed in possession of territory which might well, in other circumstances, have gravitated away from the influence of Kabul. The definition of the limits of British Baluchistan and Persian Seistan, in the process leaving territory in Afghan hands which might otherwise have been lost to the Amir, was largely the work of British boundary commissions implementing the 1893 Anglo-Afghan agreement which enshrined the Durand Line. One result was the retention within Afghanistan of Baluchi tribal groups: a fact which has caused some disturbance along this boundary in recent times.*

The ruling Afghan dynasty has good grounds for being content with its northern, western and southern boundaries. Not only did the agreements over these give Kabul more than could have been expected from the power of the government established in that city, but also the process of their creation helped to ensure stability and security. Russian control in Turkestan and British control in Baluchistan in each case established law and order in regions whence, in the past, had originated tribal raids on Afghan territory. Afghan dynasties, for example, had throughout recorded history been subject to attack and destruction from Central Asia. The presence of the Russians, once the Russo-Afghan boundary had been settled, brought

* For example: in early 1948, following the accession to Pakistan of Kalat state (the most important of the Baluchistan princely states acknowledging British paramountcy), a member of the Kalat dynasty, Karim, fled to Afghanistan where he received Afghan help in an attempt to reverse accession. The Kalat ruling families possessed close ties with families on the Afghan side of the border; and no doubt Kabul took advantage of this in its policy, which was directed ultimately, one imagines, towards the creation of an Afghan outlet to the Indian Ocean which did not pass through Pakistani territory.

that danger to an end. The Russians controlled the nomads; British frontier policy controlled the Russians and guaranteed that they would not advance below the defined boundary.

Throughout the great age of Afghan boundary-creation, the Kabul government was limited in its foreign relations by treaty with the British. In 1919, the Afghans obtained full independence at a moment when Central Asia was much disturbed by the consequences of the Russian Revolution. A Soviet-Afghan agreement of 1921 by implication created the possibility of some modification of the old Russo-Afghan border in the Panjdeh region and in the Pamirs, where, also by implication, there would be plebiscites. At the same time, Afghanistan acquired control of a small tract of Russian territory in the Kushk region. The plebiscites were never held. In 1946, a Soviet-Afghan agreement returned Kushk to Russia and confirmed the border as following the line established in tsarist times; it also dealt with questions of water-use, defined with greater precision the border along the mid-channel, or *thalweg*, of the Oxus, and decided the ownership of some islands in that river. Since 1946, despite the fact that Afghanistan has become a zone of competition between the Soviet Union and the United States, the Oxus boundary has remained stable and free of major crises. It is in the east, not in the north or south or west, that Kabul has found the imperialist-created boundary to be unsatisfactory.

The eastern boundary of modern Afghanistan lies along the hills which separate the Hindu Kush from the Indus valley. It is inhabited by Pathan tribal groups, Muslim and speaking the Pashtu language. When, in the 1830s, the British approached this region, they were presented with the choice of four frontier lines. First: they could halt their territorial expansion at the east bank of the Indus or one of its tributaries, leaving between themselves and Afghanistan the Sikh state as a buffer. The collapse of the Sikh kingdom in the years that followed the death of Ranjit Singh in 1839 made this impossible. Second: they could stop at the foot of the hills on the west bank of the

Indus. For military reasons this was impracticable. The Pathan tribes were in the habit of raiding into the plains, and the British could not afford to leave this tribal fringe outside their international border; to do so would turn every punitive operation into the raw material for a major diplomatic crisis. Third: they could enclose the tribal fringe by establishing a line along the crests of the outlying ranges of the Hindu Kush system. Fourth: they could create a line which either followed or approached the crests of the main Hindu Kush massif.

The problem of the Pathan tribes, the classic dilemma of the North-West Frontier of British India, produced much experiment. The final solution was to abandon any advanced boundary which brought the great majority of the Pathans within the British sphere. To have included within British India the bulk of the Pathan lands—to create, in other words, the so called 'scientific frontier' following the line Kabul–Kandahar—seemed to British strategists to present insuperable military problems. The history of Anglo-Afghan relations during the course of the nineteenth century convinced the government of India that it would not be practicable to take over control of the heartland of the Afghan state. Hence, the final British answer was to leave Kabul and Kandahar alone. The eastern parts of the Pathan area were enclosed within the British border, but direct British administration was not extended across a line even farther to the east along the foot of the hills. This was the Durand Line solution. It created an Afghan boundary which was for much of its length unadministered except when tribal disturbances called for punitive campaigns. It left a large Pathan population within Afghanistan.

The Durand Line was defined in principle in the Anglo-Afghan Agreement of November 1893, signed by the foreign secretary of India, Sir Mortimer Durand, and Amir Abdurrahman. Much of the line was subsequently laid down on the ground by Anglo-Afghan boundary commissions. The 1893 Agreement was confirmed by Amir Habibullah in 1905, Amir

Amanullah in 1921, and King Muhammed Nadir Shah in 1930. In deciding upon the course of the Durand Line, an attempt was made wherever possible to avoid partitioning areas occupied by particular Pathan tribal groups; and in general this was achieved. The most notable exception is, perhaps, the Mohmand country just to the north of the Khyber pass which the line cuts in half. The Durand boundary here, with the adjacent sectors to its north in Bajaur, was never demarcated in British times: a fact which has caused some trouble since 1947. In September 1960, and again in May 1961, there were armed clashes in this region between Pakistani troops and Pathan tribesmen from the Afghan side of the line.

Although the Pathans perhaps do not make up a majority of the population of Afghanistan, the Afghan dynasty is Pathan and the country can in some respects be described as a Pathan state. Since the eighteenth century, the Afghans have looked upon the Indus valley as the natural direction for their political expansion. There is still much resentment at the loss to the Sikhs in the early nineteenth century of the city of Peshawar. It is not surprising that in Kabul there should have been much thought given to the possibility of establishing a dominant Afghan influence over the Pathan tribal tracts between the Durand Line and the British administrative boundary. It seemed that an opportunity was provided by the ending of British rule in the subcontinent in 1947. Afghanistan voted against the admission of Pakistan, heir to the British on the North-West Frontier, to the United Nations. It has since then consistently denied the validity of the Durand Line. One argument has been that, since the Durand Line agreement was made solely between the Afghans and the British, it lapsed with the departure of the latter. With some covert Indian assistance, Afghanistan has agitated for the creation along the North-West Frontier of a Pathan state: Pakhtunistan. There were major crises in Afghan-Pakistani relations over this issue in 1955–57 and 1961–63.

There are a number of absurdities and contradictions in the Afghan case for Pakhtunistan, and it is clear that many of the arguments which the Afghans raised in this connection were intended for internal rather than external consumption. The control of Pakistan over the Pathan hills has never been seriously threatened; provided that the Pakistani state remains stable, it is unlikely to be so threatened. It is improbable that a majority of the Pathans inhabiting Pakistani territory have any wish to become Afghan subjects. There are almost as many Pathans in Pakistan as in Afghanistan; the head of the Pakistani state at this time, Mohammed Ayub Khan, is a Pathan. On ethnic grounds, Pakistan could perhaps raise strong arguments for the acquisition of the Pathan areas of Afghanistan.

The eastern boundary of Afghanistan marks a line across which came many of the nomadic invaders of the Indian subcontinent. With the establishment of British rule over the Indus valley, this danger finally disappeared. No Afghan force had the power to defeat a British army in the plains, though it might well secure tactical victories in the hills. The threat along the classic invasion route was not seen in the British period as tribal in character; the threat lay in the possibility that another European force, that of Russia, might secure access to the passes leading from the Hindu Kush towards the Indus. Nomads, however, continued to cross the frontier zone. The so-called *povindahs* throughout the British era wintered in the plains and passed the summer grazing in the Afghan highlands. One consequence of the crises over the validity of the Durand Line in the post-British era has been the resolve of the government of Pakistan to close the border once and for all to nomad traffic. Here, as elsewhere in Asia, the modern process of boundary-making has struck a fatal blow at the nomadic way of life, once such a crucial factor in the historical evolution of the Asian continent.

★

There are two aspects of the modern post-colonial situation on the North-West Frontier which deserve special comment here. First: the transfer of power from a colonial to an indigenous regime has not resulted, *ipso facto*, in the solution of a frontier problem. Pakistan, because it is an Islamic state with many Pathans in positions of power, has perhaps found it easier than the British to deal with the North-West Frontier tribes. It cannot, however, maintain that the North-West Frontier was a purely colonial problem. Second: the Afghan claim that the Pathans, now that British imperial rule has gone, should enjoy independence contains within it a point of great interest which relates to many of the colonial regions of Asia. It was British policy which united the Pathan hill tracts to the plains of the Indus valley. By what right should that union persist in the post-colonial era? In this particular instance, there are grounds for supposing that the union enjoys a real measure of popular support, and there is a moral basis for it in the Islamic nature of the Pakistani state. Apply this question, however, to other historically separate peoples who have been wedded by the bonds of imperial historical accident, and the answer may not be so easy to find.

5

Pakistan

Pakistan is a phenomenon unique in those regions of modern Asia which are the subject of this study; it is a state the limits of which are defined explicitly by religious criteria. With the end of the Raj in 1947, Britain's Indian empire was partitioned in such a way that the Muslim majority areas in and contiguous to Panjab and Bengal were joined together in one political entity: Pakistan. In some ways, this was a strange match. West Panjab and East Bengal, apart from Islam, had very little in common with each other. There are major ethnic and cultural differences between the two regions. Never before had there been a state in the subcontinent with anything quite like the dual boundary system of Pakistan. Indeed, only modern communications, wireless, power-driven ship and aeroplane, have made possible the political unification of two such widely separated tracts as the West and East wings of the Islamic state of Pakistan. (See Maps 13 and 14.)

The boundaries of Pakistan, as they emerged in 1947, fall into two distinct categories. First: along the western edge of West Pakistan, the new state inherited the British frontier with Iran, Afghanistan and China. The defined boundaries here separate

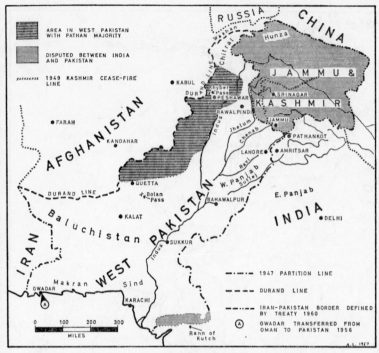

13. West Pakistan.

Islamic majorities in British India from Islamic majorities outside the British dominions. Second: along the eastern side of West Pakistan and all the way round the landward side of East Pakistan are boundaries between territories which had all been British before 1947. These boundaries also fall into two categories, namely, the boundaries between Pakistan and the Indian republic, which were the direct product of the process of partition in 1947; and the short boundary between East Pakistan and Burma. In 1937, British Burma was separated from British India, becoming a colonial territory in its own right, under the Burma Office in London (which, however, shared its secretary of state with the India Office). On April 1, 1937, the boundary between Assam and Bengal on the one

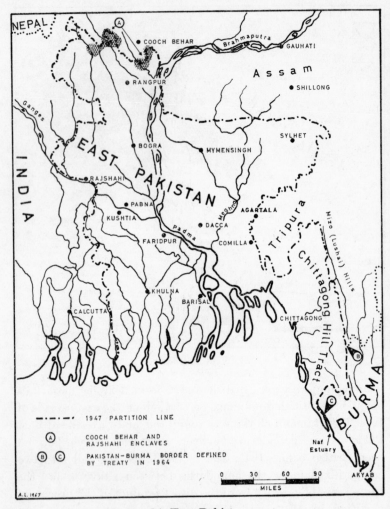

14. East Pakistan.

hand and Burma on the other ceased to be an internal boundary of the Indian empire and became a boundary between two
distinct British dependencies—like, for example, the boundary
between Kenya and the Anglo-Egyptian Sudan.

Pakistan has had to face a twofold problem on the East Pakistan-Burma border. In the first place, this line does not mark a clear ethnic divide. It evolved out of British reactions in the early nineteenth century to the expansionist tendencies of the Burmese Konbaung dynasty towards Arakan and the hill tracts of Assam and Bengal. There are over 300,000 Buddhists in Pakistan at the present time, the majority of them living in East Pakistan and possessing ties of some kind with populations in Burma. The 80,000 or so Buddhists of Chittagong and the Chittagong hill tracts, for example, are either Arakanese or members of hill tribes whose habitat extends across the Pakistan-Burma border into the Chin hills. There is a Muslim population of comparable size on the Burmese side of the boundary. These minorities have created some minor problems in Pakistani-Burmese relations. The second factor in Pakistan's problem is to be found in the precise alignment of the boundary where it follows the Naf river. The Naf has a rather variable course. Islands have appeared and disappeared in its estuary. There were sources of argument here in British times which Pakistan and the independent Burmese state have inherited. The Burmese attitude to this particular boundary has not been simplified by the sometimes tenuous nature of the control of the Burmese central government over the Arakan Yoma and the Chin hills. But there are no insuperable difficulties here, and the Memorandum of Agreement which Burma and Pakistan signed in January 1964 has provided a sound basis for their amicable settlement.

The border between India and East Pakistan is extra-ordinarily complex, running as it does across the Ganges-Brahmaputra delta. From the economic point of view, it is a very strange border indeed. In the British period, for instance, what is now East Pakistan developed into the world's major producer of jute. The mills processing this material, however, were mainly located in what, in 1947, became the republic of India. One result has been the rise since partition of an active

smuggling trade in jute from Pakistan to India, where the mills
are hungry for raw materials. Part of the eastern border of East
Pakistan touches on the Assam hills, and with the outbreak o
tribal rebellion in Indian Assam, there has been a certain
temptation for Pakistani intervention across this border. Indian
spokesmen have sometimes implied that Pakistan is aiding the
Nagas, but so far no concrete evidence that this is so has been
produced. The shape of East Pakistan as it was defined in 1947
resulted in the severing of some of the main road, rail and water
communications between West Bengal and Assam: a fact which
created a situation replete with possibility of complications in
the course of Indo-Pakistani relations in the age of independence. Finally, the 1947 partition was not without its ambigui-
ties; in the Cooch Behar region, for example, it left a number of
small enclaves of Indian and Pakistani territory on either side
of the border. All this could have produced far more trouble
than has, in fact, been the case. There have, of course, been
crises and incidents along the border between India and East
Pakistan, but none beyond control. The problems of this border
were the subject of the Noon-Nehru discussions of 1958 which,
by 1960, resolved (on paper at least) a number of problems,
including that of the enclaves of the old state of Cooch Behar.
Here was a demonstration that it was theoretically possible for
the two sovereign powers succeeding to the British Raj to come
to terms on territorial matters.*

* There have been delays in the implementation of some of the
decisions reached in 1960, notably the Pakistani right to Berubari
enclave. A section of Indian opinion has denied that the government in
Delhi has the constitutional right to cede Indian territory to a foreign
power, even when only a few square miles are involved. It is interesting
to compare India's attitude here with that of some Pakistanis over the
settlement of the Baluchistan border between Pakistan and Iran. In
both cases, there has been local opposition to territorial transfers; but
the Pakistani central authorities have been much firmer in resisting such
opposition and in proceeding to the implementation of fully negotiated
agreements.

Pakistan's most serious problem of frontier policy, there can be no doubt at all, is to be found in Kashmir. Defects in British planning resulted in a failure to arrange Kashmir's future before August 15, 1947, the date of the transfer of power in the sub-continent; and Indian and Pakistani statesmen have not found a satisfactory answer in the twenty years which have followed. Kashmir, the scene of two Indo-Pakistani wars (1947–49 and 1965), is at present uneasily divided into two portions, roughly equal in area (though not in economic importance), which are separated from each other by a heavily guarded cease-fire line. (See Map 15.)

Kashmir, or more properly, the state of Jammu and Kashmir, has a Muslim majority population which, in the British period, came under the rule of a Hindu dynasty. The state, as we now know it, was very much the creation of the Dogra ruler of Jammu, Gulab Singh, who rose to power in the early nineteenth century as a feudatory of Ranjit Singh, the builder of the Sikh kingdom of Lahore. From his dynastic base in Jammu, Gulab Singh in 1834 conquered the old Buddhist kingdom of Ladakh. The Ladakhis in race and culture were closely related to Tibet, and their rulers had for long accepted a dependent status in relation to the Tibetan and Chinese authorities in Lhasa. In 1840, Gulab Singh took over Baltistan along the Indus to the west of Ladakh: a region inhabited mainly by people of Ladakhi stock who had been converted to Islam. The union of Jammu (and its dependency Poonch) with Ladakh and Baltistan brought the power of a state in the closest of political relationships with the Indus plains right up to the Tibetan plateau and the edge of the Chinese sphere.

During the Anglo-Sikh war of 1845–46, Gulab Singh took care not to commit himself to the side of his Sikh overlords. The British rewarded him by selling him the former Sikh province in the vale of Kashmir. The Jhelum valley had once been the site of a flourishing Hindu culture, with its capital at Srinagar. In the fourteenth century, however, it was subjected to Islamic

DISPUTED BETWEEN INDIA AND CHINA

INDIA SAYS PAKISTAN SURRENDERED THIS TERRITORY TO CHINA IN 1963

••••••••• 1949 CEASE-FIRE LINE

—••—••— BORDER OF JAMMU & KASHMIR AS CLAIMED BY INDIA

••—••—• 1963 SINO-PAKISTANI BORDER

— — — EASTERN END OF BRITISH 1899 BOUNDARY PROPOSAL TO CHINA

▬▬▬ CHINESE ROAD ACROSS AKSAI CHIN

15. Kashmir.

invasion, and by the time of the Sikh conquest of the province in 1819, its population had long been converted to Islam. Its addition to Gulab Singh's dominions produced a strange union of Hindus, Sikhs, Tibetan Buddhists and Muslims in a state which had no basis in cultural tradition or political history. It was a state, however, that the British found useful in their efforts to limit the area of their direct administration in the north-west. For the remainder of the nineteenth century, the Indian government used it as a convenient receptacle for sovereignty in those regions along the upper Indus and the southern side of the main Karakoram watershed into which British influence was extended in reaction to Russian advances into Turkestan and the Pamirs. Thus, the maharaja of Jammu and Kashmir was allowed to acquire some title over Gilgit and hill states like Hunza and Nagar which British strategists thought it desirable to exclude from the potential Russian sphere.

In Jammu, Kashmir and Ladakh the British intervened as little as they could.* For a time during the late nineteenth and early twentieth centuries, the Indian government felt itself obliged to suspend the maharaja's powers; but by the end of British rule in the subcontinent, the maharaja of Jammu and Kashmir in these districts possessed more real power than that enjoyed by the ruler of any other princely state in British India. In the Gilgit region, however, where Kashmir approached the frontiers of the Russian sphere, the British limited the maharaja's influence in practice to that of a theoretical suzerainty. The frontier was too important to be allowed to pass from direct British control. By 1947, therefore, Jammu and Kashmir had, in effect, been partitioned into two zones: one under British administration exercised through a Political Agency at Gilgit, and one under the maharaja with his summer capital at Srinagar and his winter capital at Jammu.†

* In Ladakh, for instance, the main British concern was to see that the Kashmiri authorities did not obstruct the transit trade between Sinkiang and directly administered British territory.

† Chitral might possibly be considered in this context as a third zone. In 1876, the British recognised that Chitral was under the suzerainty of Kashmir; but administratively they kept Chitral, one of the states in the Malakand Agency (along with Dir and Swat), quite separate from Kashmir. The Malakand Agency was a crucial sector of the British border with Afghanistan. In October 1947, Chitral formally acceded to Pakistan. India, however, has on occasion challenged Pakistan's rights in Chitral. In May 1956, for example, Nehru informed the Lok Sabha, the lower house of the Indian Parliament, that he did not consider that

During the British period, the boundaries between Kashmir and Sinkiang and Tibet were never defined because the British were unable to decide what alignment would best suit their strategic needs. There was an obvious geographical boundary between the Gilgit area and Sinkiang along the main Karakoram watershed dividing streams flowing into the Indus basin from those flowing into the Tarim basin. For administrative purposes, the British accepted this line as their boundary, and they were content with it so long as there existed no prospect of a Russian annexation or political domination of Sinkiang.*

Chitral's status had changed since 1876—in other words, that it was still a dependency of the maharaja of Jammu and Kashmir, and therefore, by virtue of Kashmir's accession, a dependency of the Indian republic. The claim to Chitral gives India a theoretical common border with Afghanistan, but, it must be admitted, the Indians have never pressed this particular claim with much energy or enthusiasm.

* This boundary line was somewhat complicated by the existence of the state of Hunza, subordinate in theory to Kashmir and located adjacent to Chinese territory along the Karakoram. The mir, or ruler, of Hunza had entered into some kind of tributary relationship during the eighteenth century with the Chinese authorities in Kashgar. He paid to the Chinese a small annual tribute, and the Chinese presided over his installation in office. As a result of this Chinese connection, the mir of Hunza was able to maintain grazing and revenue rights to the north of the main watershed in the districts of Raskam and the Taghdumbash Pamir. In the 1890s, when Hunza was brought under British paramountcy—though still remaining under some measure of Kashmir sovereignty—the mir was reluctant to give up his rights to the north. The British, therefore, permitted him to continue paying tribute to the Chinese. It would appear that Hunza did not cease this practice until the last decade of British rule. The Hunza relationship with the Chinese gave the Kashgar authorities in Sinkiang some interest, if only rather theoretical, to the south of the main watershed. It also meant that a British-protected state maintained rights and interests to the north of the watershed. The British never managed to negotiate with China a definition of Hunza's status. The Sino-Pakistani boundary agreement of 1963, however, would seem to contain a tacit Chinese renunciation of claims over Hunza and a Pakistani renunciation of the bulk of the Hunza rights and interests north of the watershed.

However, in periods when it seemed as if the Russians might displace the Chinese in Sinkiang, the British gave thought to the extension of at least their theoretical sovereignty to the northern glacis of the Karakoram so as to keep Russia as far away as possible from the centres of Indian population. This glacis possessed few inhabitants and would require very little administration. A British boundary which embraced it would involve less the extension northwards of British rule than the extension eastwards of a buffer strip, almost a continuation of the Wakhan tract of Afghanistan which Anglo-Russian diplomacy had created in 1893–95. This strip would be part of a British-protected state, Jammu and Kashmir, and not of a British Indian province.

The nearest the British ever came to definition here was in 1899, when they proposed a boundary agreement with China embodying the watershed line and leaving in Chinese hands the northern glacis. The proposal was made at a moment when the Russian danger was thought to be on the wane. The Chinese, however, failed to make formal reply to the 1899 plan. By 1912, the Russian threat was once more waxing and a more northerly boundary seemed desirable. In the late 1920s, with the Russian danger waning again, the 1899 line was revived, only to be rejected once more in the 1930s with the rise to power in Sinkiang of Sheng Shih-t'sai who, the British were convinced, was a Russian puppet. Because they were dealing, in theory at least, with the territory of a client state, they could afford to be far vaguer than would have been possible with a British province. They could wait until the future of Sinkiang became clearer before committing themselves to any final boundary definition. The moment had not yet arrived when the British left India in 1947.

The 1899 plan not only concerned Kashmir's boundary with Sinkiang, but also part of the state's boundary with Tibet in the extreme north-eastern corner of Ladakh. Here, too, there were a number of theoretical possibilities. There was a watershed

H

line, though not so clear as it was farther to the west, and
there was a line which enclosed the northern glacis. The 1899
plan involved a watershed alignment, but there were other
possibilities farther to the north. By 1947, the British had still
not made up their minds, though they were inclined towards a
compromise alignment midway between the watershed and the
most northerly suggestions.

British uncertainty had its cartographical consequences. A
study of maps will show a wide range of boundaries in northern
Kashmir. Official maps during the last years of the Raj tended
to show no boundary at all; but where a boundary was shown,
it should cause no surprise to find that it usually lay north of the
minimum British proposals. The Chinese are not the only people
to have practised what it is now fashionable to call 'cartographical aggression'. A boundary on the map could always be
withdrawn: it would not be so easy to advance it.

In British frontier policy, the state of Jammu and Kashmir
performed a number of buffer functions. Yet, unlike Nepal and
Afghanistan, it was an integral part of the Indian empire. The
union of Jammu and Kashmir was, after all, a British creation.
In the Gilgit region, which occupied nearly one-third of the
state's area, the British by the end of the nineteenth century
enjoyed greater influence than did the maharaja's government.
In the 1930s, the Indian government actually acquired a lease
of portions of Gilgit from the maharaja; and on the eve of the
British departure, the whole of the Gilgit Agency was, in effect,
an outlying administrative district of what would soon become
West Pakistan. Although it was British policy to minimise
interference with the internal affairs of Jammu and Kashmir,
the Indian government was still obliged to involve itself to a
degree which it never attempted in states like Nepal and
Bhutan. Delhi could not escape imposing some form of constitutional government on the maharaja; the consequence,
though by no means the British intention, was to encourage the
spread into the state of the influence of the Indian nationalist

movement which was steadily gaining strength in adjacent territory under direct British administration. During the last decades of the Raj, the economy of the state of Jammu and Kashmir became increasingly integrated with that of the Panjab in British India. This was more the product of geography than policy. The result was that, by 1947, political and economic factors made it extremely unlikely that the state could hope to escape the consequences of the partition of British India between India and Pakistan.

Partition involved Jammu and Kashmir in quite a new kind of frontier problem. The state had been created and maintained as part of the British solution of the problem posed by the external frontiers of the subcontinent. As such, in 1947, it became enmeshed, and inevitably so, in the process of erection of a new frontier system within the subcontinent itself; and here the question of Anglo-Russian rivalry was, for the time being at least, irrelevant. Policy now had to be directed, not to keeping the Russians away, but to the creation of two viable successor states to the British Raj.

In the context of partition, it would be difficult to imagine a frontier policy which did not postulate Pakistani control of some at least of the territory of Jammu and Kashmir. Some of the major rivers of West Pakistan, essential to the agriculture of that region, either rise in or flow through the state. Pakistan was based on the proposition that the Muslims of British India, wherever the criterion of viability could be applied, should enjoy an independence separate from the Hindu majority. Kashmir not only had a Muslim majority but also was in direct territorial contact with the core of West Pakistan. Assuming the possibility of Indo-Pakistani hostility in the age of independence—and such an assumption would not have seemed unreasonable in the light of the Hindu-Muslim communal blood-bath which accompanied the British departure from the subcontinent—then Kashmir was vital to the defence of West Pakistan.

Jammu and Kashmir, however, because of past British frontier policy as much as anything else, was still in 1947 an Indian princely state. Its ruler, under the terms of the British proposals for Indian independence, had the right to determine his own future. After a period of delay, in October 1947, the maharaja of Jammu and Kashmir opted for India. His accession was accepted by the Indian government, partly because it too wanted the Kashmir territories for the defence of its north-west—a continuation of the old British frontier policy—and partly because it wished to punish Pakistan for its alleged attempt to force the maharaja's decision by sponsoring an invasion of the state by Pathan tribesmen from the North-West Frontier. The result was to be two wars, two cease-fires and the creation of a source of Indo-Pakistani tension which has continued unabated for twenty years.

The vast edifice of legalistic and moral argument that has been erected by both sides in the Kashmir dispute need not concern us here. In terms of frontier policy, the strongest Indian argument for the possession of Kashmir in 1947 would have been that Pakistan was unlikely to acquire sufficient political and economic stability to be able to bear the burden of the maintenance of that portion of the old British imperial frontier system which had fallen to it through partition. It would be more difficult to advance such an argument today. Pakistan still stands, and is manifestly capable of looking after its share of the old British external frontier. It can well be argued that the defences of the subcontinent have been weakened, not by Pakistani chaos, such as might have been anticipated by some observers in 1947, but by an Indian refusal to come to terms with the implications of Pakistani strength. Indo-Pakistani conflict over Kashmir—the inevitable consequence of the Indian attempt to act on the maharaja's accession in 1947—has shattered the old British frontier system, which was designed to exclude from the subcontinent all influences from the Russian and Chinese zones. The Indian republic flies Russian MIG fighter aircraft; Pakistan has in its army tanks which were made in China.

The Indo-Pakistani dispute over Kashmir has given the region a rather complex political structure. Ladakh and the bulk of Jammu, Poonch and the vale of Kashmir, including Srinagar, are in Indian hands. At the outset, Indian-held Kashmir was treated as a rather special region and distinct from the rest of India. Of late, however, it has become increasingly integrated within the fabric of the Indian republic. Pakistan holds small portions of Jammu, Poonch and Kashmir provinces as well as the bulk of Baltistan and the Gilgit region. Three districts—Mirpur (once part of Jammu), Poonch (which is the smaller part of the old Poonch province) and Muzaffarabad (once part of Kashmir province), are now Azad (Free) Kashmir with its capital at Muzaffarabad town. Azad Kashmir is not formally part of Pakistan, though very closely related to the Pakistani government through the latter's Ministry of Kashmir Affairs. Gilgit and Baltistan are now two Political Agencies which, like Azad Kashmir, are not formally Pakistani territory though administered by Pakistan through the Resident for Gilgit and Baltistan: an official who also holds the position of secretary to the Ministry of Kashmir Affairs. Within the Gilgit Agency are the states of Hunza and Nagar which, to add further complexity to an already complex situation, have formally acceded to Pakistan. Thus has the former British frontier tract of Kashmir become fragmented.

As a frontier zone, Kashmir concerns not only India and Pakistan but also China, which marches with the north and north-east of the state. It was inevitable, therefore, that Kashmir should become involved in the Sino-Indian boundary crisis and that attention should be focused on the external boundaries here which the British left undefined. In 1963, China and Pakistan agreed to a boundary along the main Indus-Tarim watershed in the Karakoram which corresponded very closely to the line proposed by the British in 1899. India, however, has refused to accept anything like the 1899 proposals in north-eastern Ladakh. This is perhaps unfortunate, since the main Chinese interest in the region, the road from Sinkiang to Tibet across the Aksai Chin plateau, lies outside the 1899 line.* Indian resistance here, however, is easy to understand; and one of its causes, there can be no doubt, is the reluctance to surrender to anyone any territory which could in theory be described as part of the state of Jammu and Kashmir. To do so would be to weaken the Indian case *vis à vis* Pakistan.

Kashmir is only one example, though by far the most important, of the way in which frontier policy was not applied as realistically as it might have been by the British in 1947 when they were splitting into two sovereignties their Indian empire. British India was a complex structure of states, agencies and provinces subdivided into districts. It did not reflect with any precision in its internal boundaries the religious criterion of the 1947 partition. The Indian economy, moreover, as it had evolved under British rule, did not always lend itself to easy division on these lines. It was inevitable that the Radcliffe Commission which worked out the lines of partition should have had to adopt in places compromise solutions, the wisdom of which was capable of later questioning. Should Gurdaspur district in the Panjab, with a Muslim majority and contiguous to territory placed in Pakistan, have gone to India?† Would it

* It has been argued that the Chinese road cuts across the extreme eastern end of the 1899 line and, therefore, involves an intrusion into a small sector of territory which would have been Indian even if the 1899 proposals had become the accepted international boundary. The author cannot agree with this argument, which is based on a misunderstanding of the cartographical principles on which the 1899 line was defined.

† The award of the Gurdaspur district to India has given rise to much ill feeling in Pakistan, where it is pointed out that only through Gurdaspur did India acquire a viable road communication with Kashmir. Had Gurdaspur gone to Pakistan, India could hardly have maintained its forces on Kashmiri soil. Pakistanis often see in the Gurdaspur award evidence of secret British collusion with India on the Kashmir question. The evidence, which is by no means clear and satisfactory, rather sug-

not have been wiser to give Tripura, and even the Lushai hills, to Pakistan rather than to India? Could not the peculiar mosaic of sovereignties along the East Pakistan-West Bengal boundary have been better sorted out? Should not some more thought have been given to the Rann of Kutch?

There is not space here to go into these questions in detail. The main point is that the process of partition was dominated by the communal issue to such a degree that more general, and long-term, considerations of frontier policy were forgotten. The boundaries of Pakistan and India had to separate not only different religious majority areas but also two sovereign states. If the boundaries were unsatisfactory *qua* boundaries, regardless of their merits on religious grounds, then they were bound to cause trouble in the future. The extension of India into Tripura and the Lushai hills, for example, is a geopolitical absurdity. It is hard to justify, on purely political grounds, an Indo-Pakistani boundary in the region of the Rann of Kutch which runs along the Pakistani foreshore.* It is as if the French

gests that the Gurdaspur decision of the Radcliffe Commission was made with no thought to the Kashmir question. The point, it seems likely, was to ensure that the Indo-Pakistani border did not cut across the line of canals supplying the Indian city of Amritsar. In the event, however, it is not difficult to argue that the Gurdaspur award had most unfortunate consequences.

* The Rann of Kutch is a vast expanse of saline mud flats which, flooded during the monsoon, forms an intrusion of the Arabian Sea between Sind and Kutch state. There are in the Rann a few small islands which are permanently dry; otherwise the region is unpopulated. It has slight economic value as a source of salt, and it provides some areas of rather poor grazing. In British times, the status of the Rann was unsettled, Kutch state laying claim to it and the authorities of Sind province taking care not to prejudice by administrative acts an issue which they regarded as being *sub judice*. The majority of British maps showed the Kutch-Sind border as running along the edge of the Thar desert, though towards the end of the British period such maps also indicated that this boundary was 'disputed'. The border along the edge of the Thar desert, of course, was never intended to serve as an international boundary.

boundary with England followed the high-tide line of the Brighton and Eastbourne beaches. Even if the great Kashmir crisis—itself to a great extent a product of British failure to think along realistic political lines—had not poisoned Indo-Pakistani relations, there can be no doubt that questions such as these would still have given rise to tension between the two states. Without Kashmir, however, the chances for amicable settlement would certainly have been better.

To a very considerable degree, the boundaries between India and Pakistan must be regarded as a legacy from the British, who alone had the power in 1947 to lay down the detailed basis for partition. Indeed, some writers have given it as their opinion that the very need for partition was the product of British policy. Had the British, it is said, not tried to rule the sub-continent by dividing Muslim from Hindu, an undivided India could have taken over from the Raj. There is not space here to discuss this view. It is worth noting, however, that in the last analysis the partition of British India derived from a frontier problem which antedated British rule by several millennia. Islam came to the subcontinent as a result of foreign invasion across the North-West Frontier. It took firm root in the Indian plains nearest that frontier, as one would expect. It also took root in other regions where the divisive nature of Indian society made the new religion attractive on social grounds. Such appears to have been the case in East Bengal. The fragmented nature of Indian social structure, and the failure of Indian states to resist external attack from the north-west—these also are facets of the frontier history of the subcontinent. From them derives the general outline, though not the precise details, of the boundaries of West and East Pakistan.

6

India

Like Pakistan, India came into being as an independent state in 1947. At that time, again like Pakistan, it acquired boundaries which had no exact coincidence with those of any pre-colonial state in the subcontinent. With two exceptions, India had never produced anything like a united empire before British times. The first of the exceptions, the Maurya empire as it was expanded by Asoka in the third century BC, is known from rather unsatisfactory evidence. The extent of the Asokan state is equated with the distribution of Asokan rock and pillar inscriptions. On this basis, it can be argued that Asoka did not go as far south as the British did, but that he went farther westwards into Afghanistan than the British Raj. Such, at least, is the implication of the Asokan inscription, in Greek script and language, recently discovered near Kandahar. The second of the exceptions is the Moghul empire during the sixteenth and seventeenth centuries AD. The Moghuls, like Asoka, at the height of their power went farther west and not quite so far south as the British. The Moghul dynasty, moreover, was of non-Indian origin. Babur, its founder, was a Turk from Central Asia and a direct descendant of the great Tamerlane. The

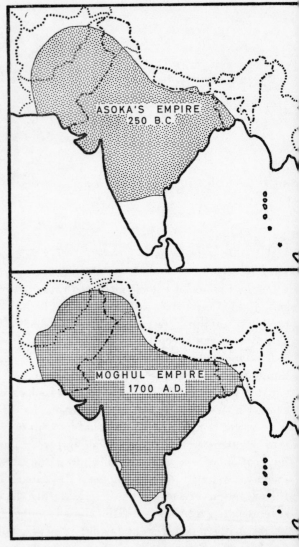

16. The limits of some Indian empires. Note that the
Gupta and Moghul empires,

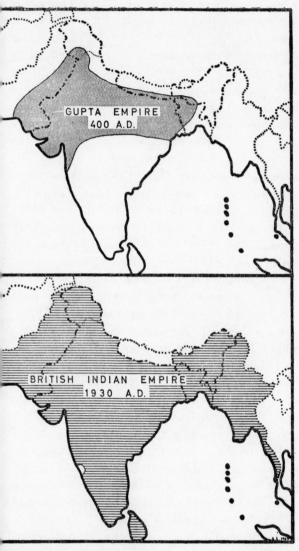

xact correspondence between the borders of the Asokan,
e of the British Raj.

Moghul empire was in many respects as foreign a regime as the British Raj. Its basis was that of Islamic rule over a non-Islamic majority. (See Map 16.)

While it may be hard to produce traditional indigenous parallels for the British Raj, there can be no doubt that Hindu states have existed in the subcontinent for a long time and that they have had their effect upon the boundary structure of the modern Indian republic. Such states, however, have tended to influence internal rather than external boundaries. In the Dravidian south, for example, the federal states of Kerala, Mysore and Madras can trace their origins to the Chera dynasty of the Malabar coast, the Hoysala dynasty of the Mysore uplands, and the Pallava, Chola and subsequent dynasties of the Tamil country. These states, now and in the past, have been based on language groups which may perhaps be taken as the indicators of distinct regional identities. Language still remains a crucial factor in the evolution of a sense of national identity in the Indian republic; and any attempts to impose the northern Sanscritic language of Hindu upon the members of the Dravidian group—the speakers of Tamil, Telegu, Kannada and Malayalam—cannot fail to strain severely the unity of the Indian federal republic.

It may be said, therefore, that the British constructed a frontier system which placed within it a number of language groups that, beyond a shared tradition of Hindu civilisation, had not hitherto possessed a long and continuous history of political unification. In doing this, perhaps, the British were following in the footsteps of the Moghuls, themselves of foreign origin. If we ignore Asoka, however, it cannot be said that the Raj coincided even remotely with something which Indians had achieved before. Even the significance of the Hindu element, and that of its Buddhist and Jain offsprings, can perhaps be exaggerated. The Hindu civilisation is certainly no less subject to regional variation than, let us say, is the civilisation of Western Christendom with its roots in the world of the Roman empire. Few today would advance the Roman empire as a rational basis for the resurrection of a united European empire. If the Indian republic fails, as some observers think it probably will fail, to make good the British frontier system, then it is likely that the internal Indian boundaries, dividing language regions and local identities, will more and more acquire the force and significance of international boundaries. In June 1966, there was a boundary dispute between the Indian states of Mysore and Maharashta (Bombay) which produced riots and loss of life. Perhaps this is a portent for the future.

It may be said that the Raj brought about the political union of diverse and hitherto separate regions within the Hindu sphere. It did so by a twofold process. First: the Hindu heartland was occupied. Second: the centres of Hindu civilisation (and, in the north-west, former Hindu regions which had come under Islamic domination) were surrounded by a frontier belt stretching from the Arabian Sea to the hills of northern Burma. Within this belt there were populations who were either marginally within or totally without the Hindu world. Many of the inhabitants of the hill tracts along the Tibetan border were Buddhist, and hence belonged to a culture which was of Indian origin; but they also possessed a long history of cultural and political ties with Tibet, which region certainly fell within the gravitational field of the Chinese empire. Some of the peoples of the frontier belt had never come under Hindu influence at all. Assam provides a number of examples of this last category.

The expansion of British power towards Burma resulted in the annexation of the hill tracts of Assam, where lived tribes belonging to the sphere of mainland South-east Asia rather than the Indian subcontinent. The peoples of the Assam Himalayas (like the Abors, Mishmis and Apa Tanis), the peoples of hills along the southern edge of the Brahmaputra valley (like the Khasis), and the peoples of the Burmese frontier tracts (like the Nagas and the Mizos [Lushais])—none of these could be described as Indian if that term were to be defined on the basis of culture. British rule, moreover, served if anything to widen the gulf between this category of tribesmen and the settled populations of the Indo-Aryan and Dravidian plains. Many of the hillmen of the North-East Frontier came under the influence of European and American Christian missionaries. They acquired a sense of their own cultural and national identity, and came to see British rule as a protection for that identity. Some of them much regretted the British departure; in the age of independence in the subcontinent, they sought to establish to a varying degree their own independence from the successors to the Raj. Here is to be found the origins of the Naga rebellion against the Indian republic.

The new Indian state, however, was in fact influenced by precisely those considerations of frontier policy which had brought the British into the tribal hills in the first place. Frontier policy dictated that Indian control should be retained over frontier tracts; the aspirations of the hill tribes against India, though essentially similar to the past aspirations of Indian nationalists against the British, had to be opposed, by force if persuasion failed (as it did in the case of the Nagas and, more recently, the Mizos).

In its struggle with the Nagas the Indian central government has not only been concerned with the security of an external frontier but also with the problem of internal separatist tendencies. Concessions to the Nagas could well create a precedent for concessions to the Sikhs or the Tamils. Such a precedent was already established in 1947, when the subcontinent was partitioned between India and Pakistan, and from that moment the government of India made it an axiom that no further partitions should take place. The theoretical basis for the 1947 partition was challenged. India declared itself a secular state and not a Hindu state.* It consisted of a multitude of races, tribes, languages and sects, and membership of any one of these

---

* A secular state, however, which had in its written Constitution a provision urging, if not actually commanding, the protection of cows.

was not, in itself, sufficient ground for a claim to the right to exist outside the Indian fold. The Indian fight for unity—to a great extent a reflection of the artificial nature of the British Raj—goes far to explain many aspects of modern Indian policy, foreign as well as internal. It lies at the root of the struggle with Pakistan over Kashmir, and it is certainly a vital factor in the attitude of New Delhi towards Chinese boundary and territorial claims in the Himalayas and the Karakoram.*

British frontier policy failed to produce a comprehensive definition of external boundaries along the Karakoram and Himalayan ranges. An extremely short stretch of boundary between Tibet and the British protectorate of Sikkim was delimited in the Anglo-Chinese Convention of 1890, but the Tibetans managed to frustrate attempts at joint Anglo-Chinese demarcation. A much longer section of boundary—the so-called McMahon Line—from Bhutan to Burma along the crest of the Assam Himalayas, was defined in a secret exchange of notes between the British and the Tibetans in March 1914 during the course of the Simla Conference. The validity of this transaction, however, is certainly open to question, and the Chinese have consistently, in both Kuomintang and Maoist times, refused to be bound by it. They deny that Tibet ever possessed the requisite treaty-making powers. For the remainder of the present Sino-Indian border—some 1,000 miles of it—there exists no formal Anglo-Chinese or Anglo-Tibetan settlement, though here and there minor boundary decisions were made informally in discussions between British and Tibetan officials.

In the terminology of the great Sino-Indian argument, which began in the 1950s, the Sino-Indian border has been divided

---

* During 1966, however, the Indian government found itself obliged to depart from a number of axiomatic principles of the Nehru era. The Sikhs have been given what amounts to a state of their own, based on special religious criteria. Concessions have been made to Hindu extremists which would imply some weakening of secularism. There has been discussion of special federal arrangements to deal with tribal problems in Assam.

into three sectors. First: there is the Western Sector, which concerns, in effect, the boundary between Ladakh in north-east Kashmir and Chinese territory in Sinkiang and Tibet. Second: there is the Middle Sector, which relates to the border in that part of the Himalayas through which the river Sutlej flows on its way from the Tibetan plateau to the Indus valley; this sector

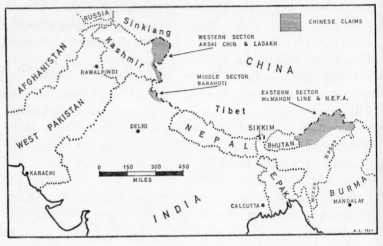

17. The Sino–Indian boundary.

stretches from Kashmir to Nepal. Third: there is the Eastern Sector, from Bhutan to Burma in the Assam Himalayas through which runs the McMahon Line. In fact, there can now be said to be a fourth: the Sikkim Sector—very short, but the scene of much tension when the second Kashmir war was at its height in the autumn of 1965. Each of these sectors had a rather different history in the British period, and the problems posed by them severally are by no means uniform. (See Maps 17, 18 and 19.)

The Western Sector is the product of British policy towards the state of Jammu and Kashmir, which possessed a common frontier with Tibet by virtue of Gulab Singh's conquest of

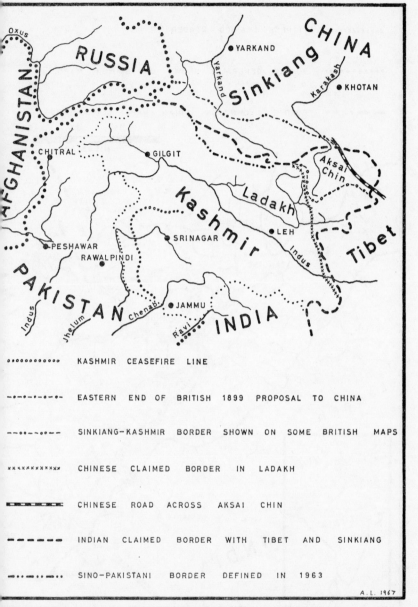

KASHMIR CEASEFIRE LINE

EASTERN END OF BRITISH 1899 PROPOSAL TO CHINA

SINKIANG–KASHMIR BORDER SHOWN ON SOME BRITISH MAPS

CHINESE CLAIMED BORDER IN LADAKH

CHINESE ROAD ACROSS AKSAI CHIN

INDIAN CLAIMED BORDER WITH TIBET AND SINKIANG

SINO–PAKISTANI BORDER DEFINED IN 1963

A.L. 1967

The western sector of the Sino-Indian boundary, showing alignments of
border between Kashmir and China as shown on British, Chinese and
Indian maps.

I

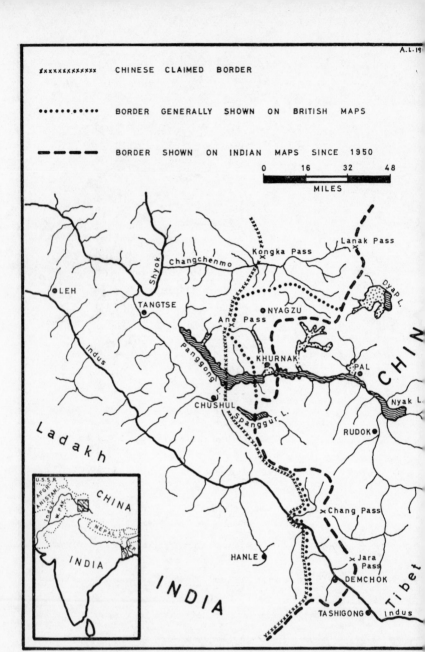

19. The Ladakh-Tibet border south of the Aksai Chin in the region
Panggong Lake and the Indus valley, showing differences between the li▸
shown on British and contemporary Indian maps.

Ladakh in 1834, and which evolved a common frontier with Chinese Turkestan (Sinkiang) during the latter part of the nineteenth century. We have already noted that the British saw the Sinkiang-Kashmir border as part of their defensive system against Russian influence. As it appeared more or less likely that the Russians would take over Sinkiang, so the British veered between advanced and moderate boundary alignments. The 1899 proposals were typical of the moderate line. By 1947, the British had not made up their minds which line to select, though they had kept their freedom of choice by either omitting external boundaries from their maps or indicating rather advanced ones. In the 1950s, the Indian republic published maps showing a Sinkiang-Kashmir boundary which was, in effect, a compromise between the British extremes. It included in India more territory than the 1899 line; but it adumbrated a rather smaller India than that suggested by the majority of British maps indicating boundary lines in this region.

In deciding on the post-1950 boundary (product of a unilateral compromise decision, and based on no firm traditions), the Indian government does not appear to have consulted the Chinese. It became clear in New Delhi in the late 1950s that the Chinese had their own ideas on boundary lines, their claims in this region being of the same general type as the line suggested to them by the British in 1899. It is possible that Sino-Indian negotiation in the 1950s might have secured the delimitation and demarcation of a boundary following the watersheds the British had indicated in 1899. The result would have been to put on the Chinese side the Sinkiang-Tibet motor road across the Aksai Chin plateau (the construction of which appears to have begun in the early 1950s but to have escaped official Indian notice until 1957). This road seems to be the major Chinese interest in this desolate quarter. Negotiations along these lines, however, were not attempted. Instead, the Indians felt themselves called upon to make 'protective' gestures in the direction of the Chinese road, to which the Chinese reacted with 'defensive' measures. What seemed 'defensive' in Peking appeared 'aggressive' in New Delhi.

The Aksai Chin plateau is a kind of no-man's-land where Sinkiang, Tibet and Indian-held Kashmir meet. South of the Aksai Chin area, along the upper reaches of the river Indus, the Kashmir-Tibet border reaches a region with a few, though small, centres of settled population, and here a traditional boundary of sorts has evolved over the centuries. It was the subject of agreement between Ladakh and Tibet in 1684 and 1842. No full demarcation ever took place (though some boundary points were established), and no maps resulted. The alignment, however, was in the British period subject only to a few very minor disputes: product of a process of Kashmiri encroachment on territory which the Tibetans regarded as theirs. It should not be forgotten that, in 1841, the founder of the Jammu and Kashmir state tried to annex the greater part of western Tibet. Military defeat did not terminate all Kashmiri ambitions in this quarter. From the 1860s, official British maps show a boundary between Kashmir and Tibet south of the Aksai Chin region which remained unmodified up to 1947. This alignment places within India some small areas which the Chinese claim should be within Tibet. It is interesting, however, that the Indian claim which was published in the 1950s placed within India some small tracts which the British, to judge by their maps, accepted as being Tibetan. It would seem that the Indian republic, once it had established itself as the protector of Kashmir against Pakistan, also found itself supporting Kashmiri claims to Tibetan territory which the British had never countenanced. The Chinese, likewise, once in control of Tibet appear to have inherited some old claims. The area involved in the discrepancies between the Chinese claim and the accepted British line is about the same as that between the British and Indian lines. It is small, but the fact that it exists should not be forgotten when considering the nature of

Chinese 'aggression' along this particular stretch of frontier.

The Middle Sector dispute can be traced without difficulty to the British period. It concerns a portion of the Himalayas—from the Sutlej valley to the present Nepalese boundary—which had been conquered by the Gurkhas of Nepal in the late eighteenth century and then annexed by the British at the end of the Anglo-Nepalese war in 1816. There were a number of minor conflicts between British and Tibetan jurisdictions along the Himalayan crest; these the British chose to ignore. The Chinese, when they became the masters of Tibet in 1951, took over the established Tibetan view of the territorial limits of Tibet along the Middle Sector. It is clear that some discussion is called for before this view can be reconciled with that now held in New Delhi and inherited from the Raj.

On the Sikkim Sector of the Sino-Indian border, more will be said in the next chapter. (See page 131.) It must suffice here to remark that the dispute which arose in 1963, and which provoked crises in 1965 and 1967, concerns an area of a few acres at the most. The Sikkim-Tibet boundary was defined in the Anglo-Chinese Convention of 1890 as following a specified watershed. The Chinese do not dispute the validity of the 1890 agreement, though they regard it as a product of the era of 'unequal treaties'. What they claim is that the Indians have built 'military structures' just on the Chinese side of the watershed at certain passes leading from Sikkim to the Chumbi valley in Tibet. Whether the Indians have, in fact, done what the Chinese allege is by no means clear. It is, in any case, probably unimportant in itself, for this dispute is almost entirely psychological. The Chinese have used it to put diplomatic pressure on the Indians. The Indians—if indeed they have erected the alleged 'military structures'—can only have done so to keep a crisis going with the minimum of risk, thereby supporting their propaganda, both for internal and external consumption, on the Chinese threat.

The final sector of the Sino-Indian border is that along which runs the famous McMahon Line. Until 1910, the government of British India considered that its international boundary east-wards of Bhutan ran along the foot of the Himalayan range on the northern side of the Brahmaputra valley. This boundary, known as the Outer Line, was laid down on the ground for some of its length by British officials in the 1870s. For a few miles east of Bhutan, it marched with what was regarded as the Tibetan district of Tawang. Further east, it separated British territory from the hill tracts occupied by tribes over which neither India nor Tibet exercised sovereignty. Where the Brahmaputra makes its great bend through the Himalayan range to become, upstream, the Tsangpo (the main river of central Tibet), the Outer Line ended; and eastwards from it there was no established boundary at all. By 1910, the Tibetans had also established a boundary of sorts along the Assam Himalayas. In Tawang, this boundary extended down through the mountains to the edge of the Assam plains. Elsewhere, it ran more or less along the crest of the range, with Tibetan influence of one kind or another extending southwards for some distance down the Subansiri, the Siang (as the Brahmaputra is known in the upper part of its passage through the Himalayas) and the Lohit rivers. However, in no case, except that of Tawang, could the Tibetans be said to have extended their influence, let alone their boundary, right down to the British Outer Line; and a buffer tract of extremely difficult mountain country, inhabited by warlike tribes, separated India from Tibet.

In 1910, China undertook the military occupation of Lhasa. This was the product of the final stage of Manchu policy in Central Asia, when an attempt was made to include Tibet within the Chinese provincial structure. Once in Tibet in force, the Chinese began to penetrate into the upper regions of the Assam hills. The British reaction was immediate. By 1914, it had been decided to move the Outer Line northwards, so that the southern slopes of the Assam Himalayas were included within the theoretical limits of British India. The collapse of Chinese power in Tibet in 1912, following the outbreak of the Chinese Revolution of 1911, provided the opportunity for this advance of the boundary. During the Simla Conference (October 1913 to July 1914), when British, Chinese and Tibetan delegates assembled to discuss the future status of Tibet in the light of the consequences of the Chinese Revolution, the British negotiated with the Tibetans a new border in Assam: the McMahon Line. It was confirmed by an exchange of secret British and Tibetan notes, and was delimited on a map not published until 1961.

In general, the McMahon Line boundary marked a reasonable limit to Tibetan sovereignty. Only in Tawang was a Tibetan area of any size transferred to the Indian empire; and even in this case, the British by 1947 had made no serious attempt to extend their administration to the northward part of Tawang, where Tibetan government continued its traditional pattern until 1951.* (See Map 20.) Elsewhere along the Himalayan crest, small pockets of territory were placed in the British sphere to which the Tibetans could lay some claim, but these were of no great significance. If there had to be a defined boundary between India and Tibet, then, except perhaps in

---

* Tawang may be divided into two regions: Tawang proper, and an area to the south of this. Tawang proper, immediately adjacent to the Tibetan border, is the seat of an important monastery with close connections with the Drebung monastery in Lhasa. Here the governors of the Tibetan district of Tsona were accustomed to make their winter capital. South of Tawang proper, beyond the Se La pass, lay a tribal tract extending down to the Assam plains which had long been under the administration of the Tawang monastery. At the close of the British period, in 1945 or 1946, Tawang up to the Se La pass was brought under the direct control of the government of India. It was not until 1951, however, that Indian administration replaced that of Tibet in Tawang proper, north of the Se La pass. During the discussion of the McMahon Line in 1914, the British at one point considered making the Se La pass the border; there can be no doubt that the Tibetans would have preferred such an alignment to the actual course of the McMahon Line, which put the whole of Tawang on the British side.

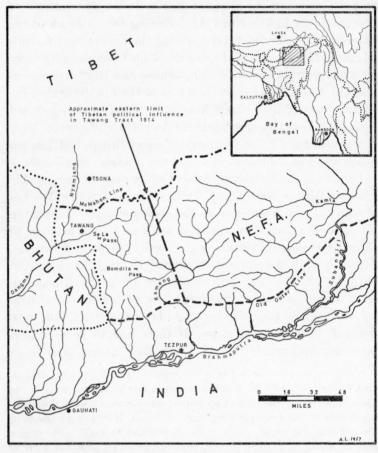

20. The Tawang tract in the Assam Himalayas.

the case of Tawang, it could hardly follow an alignment more satisfactory than that of the McMahon Line. The objection to the McMahon Line, which both the Kuomintang and the Chinese communists have raised, derives not so much from its geographical location as from its treaty basis.

The Manchu dynasty of China in the eighteenth century, as part of its Central Asian frontier policy, established a protectorate over Tibet. It claimed that it alone could represent Tibet in relations with foreign powers. Although, by the end of the nineteenth century, the effective power of China in Tibet was minimal, the British nevertheless found it convenient to recognise Chinese rights there. In Anglo-Chinese treaty relations, Tibet was Chinese: a most inconvenient fact when, in 1912, the Chinese were forced to withdraw from Central Tibet and the Tibetans wished to declare their independence.

It was not only in Anglo-Chinese treaties that the Chinese position in Tibet was confirmed. In 1904, following Lord Curzon's conviction that Russian influence over the Dalai Lama had been established, was increasing and ought to be diminished, a British expedition under Colonel Francis Younghusband was sent to Lhasa. The resultant Anglo-Tibetan treaty in effect placed Tibet to some degree under British protection. The Russians protested. The British thereupon felt themselves obliged to affirm that they had but the most limited interests in Tibet; and in 1907, in the Anglo-Russian Convention, the two imperial powers agreed to have no political relations with Tibet except through the Chinese. The British home government, unwilling to turn Tibet into a protectorate, preferred it to remain in some way under Chinese control rather than to become independent and thus free to enter into relations with the Russians. From that time until 1947, the British remained committed to the position that Tibet was in some way Chinese. The Indian republic inherited this particular legacy. In 1954, they recognised Tibet as being the 'Tibet Region of China'.

After 1917, with the fall of the tsarist regime in Russia, the British were freed from the restrictions of the 1907 Convention, and thereafter they had no hesitation in carrying on diplomatic relations with Lhasa without first consulting the Chinese. Tibet was seen as a region with some vague connection with China but with freedom to conduct its own internal and external policy. One manifestation of this freedom, the British felt, was the McMahon Line agreement of March 1914. The Chinese did

not agree, denying that Tibet had any treaty-making powers
whatsoever. The McMahon Line, however suitable as a boundary, was not based on any valid treaty, and China refused to
acccept it. The Chinese might perhaps renegotiate the McMahon
Line with independent India; they would never accept the
validity of the Anglo-Tibetan notes of 1914 or any of the other
agreements to emerge from the Simla Conference of 1913–14, all
of which they had repudiated.

The unsatisfactory nature of the treaty basis of the McMahon
Line never caused the British much anxiety. China was weak,
the victim of civil war and foreign attack. The McMahon Line
worked well enough in practice. The British, therefore, made no
attempt to create a treaty basis for this boundary (any more
than they did for the northern boundaries of Kashmir) such as
could meet the challenge of a powerful China. The Indian
republic failed, during the Sino-Indian honeymoon of the early
1950s, to remedy this defect in the frontier system which it had
inherited from the British. Later it found itself unable to do so.

From the moment of its birth, the Indian republic was faced
with what was essentially a frontier problem of formidable
proportions: Kashmir. Before the new state was ten years old,
to Kashmir had been added the intractable Sino-Indian boundary dispute. By the middle 1960s, both these questions had
involved India in major military operations; and by this time
the two issues had become inextricably entangled in the triangle
of relationships among India, Pakistan and the Chinese
People's Republic. Kashmir and the Sino-Indian border have
come to dominate not only Indian policy but also every other
aspect of Indian national planning. Yet, in themselves, neither
Kashmir nor the Sino-Indian border are major threats to
Indian security. Had it been possible in 1947 to arrive at a more
satisfactory answer for Kashmir's future status, and had it been
possible before the end of British rule to obtain a properly
negotiated boundary with Sinkiang and Tibet, then it can well
be argued that India would have been spared the consequences

of both issues. India might not, without Kashmir, have been the best of friends with Pakistan, but Indo-Pakistani hostility would certainly have been expressed in a rather different—and possibly less intense—manner. Even without the Sino-Indian boundary dispute, China and India might not have continued the much vaunted 2,000 years of brotherly friendship (based, if it existed at all, on a long history of virtual non-contact), but it is probable that Sino-Indian tensions would not have departed from the realm of verbal pronouncements.

A colonial power might well have found solutions for both problems if only because it could have possessed the freedom of action to make territorial concessions. The British Raj could, for example, have handed back part of the Tawang region to Tibet at almost any time between 1914 and 1947, simply because the region concerned was not a bit of England; and Indian public opinion would have been extremely unlikely to have taken any note of what was happening. Had China been powerful in Tibet during this period, then some such concession might well have been an acceptable Chinese price for the recognition of the McMahon Line boundary. The moment India became an independent state, its leaders were to find it far harder, even had they so desired, to justify such a cession, however advantageous its consequences.

If partition of the subcontinent had been the devising of a new administrative structure within the British empire, rather than the creation of two independent states, then, given the will to do so, it is possible that a stable settlement of the status of Kashmir could have been arrived at. There would certainly have been trouble—just as there was a great deal of trouble over Lord Curzon's partition of Bengal in 1905—but it would probably have been the kind of trouble which a strong colonial regime could have dealt with had it so wished. It can be argued —and some Indian patriots do so argue—that it would have been much better if the transfer of power in the subcontinent had been planned with more care and had taken place in stages.

The first step would have been the definition of the territorial limits of India and Pakistan; and only after these limits had become stable and effective boundaries, with their inherent problems sorted out, would sovereignty over them have been handed over to the successor regimes to the British. All this, of course, is mere speculation in the realms of what might have been. As it is, the British did not so act, and there is little evidence to suggest that they ever thought of so acting.

Once sovereignty in the subcontinent had been transferred, territorial and boundary questions acquired a new dimension. In British eyes, both Kashmir and the Sino-Indian (or Indo-Tibetan) border had been essentially imperial frontier questions. In Indian and Pakistani eyes, they became questions relating to the integrity of the sacred soil of the motherland: questions with an overwhelmingly high emotional content. It is unlikely that Pakistani public opinion would ever countenance the abandonment of claims to Kashmir, however sensible this might be on diplomatic or economic grounds. It is unlikely that any Indian government will now find it easy to hand over territory to the Chinese—even tracts totally uninhabited, like the Aksai Chin—because to do so would be interpreted by Indian public opinion as the surrender of the Hindu soil of Mother India.

These unresolved territorial and boundary questions must weigh very heavily on the negative side of the balance of the British legacy to India and Pakistan; and in the long run they may well turn out to cancel many of the positive achievements of the colonial era.

7

The Himalayan States:
Nepal, Sikkim and Bhutan

By the end of the eighteenth century, the expanding British possessions in the Indian subcontinent had already reached the fringes of the Himalayan range. During the course of the nineteenth century, British influence penetrated all but the most easterly stretches of the Himalayas; and in some places—Kumaon provides an example—direct British administration was extended to the very edge of the Tibetan plateau, which the government in Delhi regarded as being in some way part of the Chinese world. Along the Himalayas, however, three tracts remained outside the sphere of direct British government, though all three were brought to some degree under British protection. The modern history of these three regions—Nepal, Sikkim and Bhutan—has played an important part in the evolution of Sino-Indian relations, for here are potential or actual buffers along a frontier zone of acute international tension. Both the physical limits and the internal administration of modern Nepal, Sikkim and Bhutan (often referred to collectively as the Himalayan states) were to a great extent determined by the operation of British policy, even if at times it

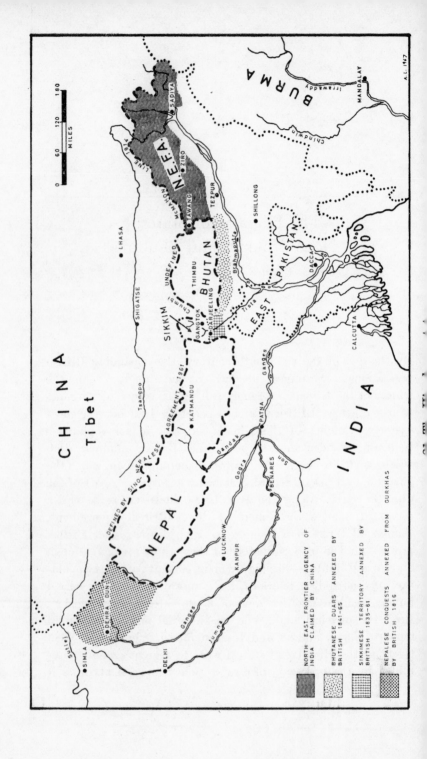

NORTH EAST FRONTIER AGENCY OF
INDIA CLAIMED BY CHINA

BHUTANESE DUARS ANNEXED BY
BRITISH 1841-65

SIKKIMESE TERRITORY ANNEXED BY
BRITISH 1835-61

NEPALESE CONQUESTS ANNEXED FROM GURKHAS
BY BRITISH 1816

was a policy of omission rather than commission. The nature of their relationships to the Indian republic is very much part of the legacy of the British Raj. (See Map 21.)

NEPAL

The present Nepalese state has its origins in the middle of the eighteenth century, when the Gurkhas—a Hindu clan from the eastern part of the country—conquered the Nepalese vale, with its three cities of Katmandu, Pathan and Bhatgaon. The vale had up to that time been ruled by the Newars: Buddhist dynasties with close relations with the authorities in central Tibet. Through the Newar territory ran the main channel of trade between the Tibetan plateau and the Gangetic plains. With the Gurkha conquest, there was a marked deterioration in Tibeto-Nepalese relations and a serious decline in that trade upon which the wealth of the vale greatly depended. Tensions with a strong economic basis created a period of crisis from 1788 to 1792, when the Gurkhas twice attacked Tibetan territory and thereby provoked Chinese intervention on behalf of the Tibetans. The Gurkhas, while more than a match for the Tibetans, were unable to deal with a large Chinese force of the kind which the Manchus in the late eighteenth century still had the power and resources to deploy on remote frontier tracts. Faced with the prospect of Chinese invasion, the Gurkhas made their peace and accepted the status of Chinese tributary, with the obligation to send a mission to Peking once in every five years.

Frustrated to the north by the Chinese, the Ghurkas began to expand to the west, east and south, occupying much of the hill country between the present western border of Nepal and the Sutlej valley, threatening Sikkim and Bhutan, and encroaching on to the plains along the northern edge of the Ganges valley. Inevitably, they came into conflict with states on the fringes of the then expanding British Indian possessions. The result was the Anglo-Nepalese war of 1814–16. British victory was followed by some definition of Nepalese boundaries. The

Gurkha hill conquests to the west, in Kumaon and Garwhal, were taken over by the British; a limit was drawn to Nepalese influence to the south, in the low-lying tracts known as the Terai; and Sikkim was taken under British protection in order to hem in the Gurkhas to the east. A British Residency was established at Katmandu and the Indian government acquired some control over Nepalese foreign relations. Because of the extant Sino-Nepalese connection, however, the British made no attempt to annex the core of the Gurkha dominions as they had existed in 1792, when the Chinese established their 'protection' over the Katmandu authorities. In Calcutta, then the capital of British India, there was considerable anxiety lest interference in this portion of the Chinese sphere might produce reprisals against British trade at Canton on the China coast. For this reason, the British resolved upon a policy of non-interference in Nepalese internal affairs. Their Resident at Katmandu was, in effect, restricted in his freedom of movement to the vale. Even when, in the latter part of the nineteenth century, Gurkha mercenaries began to play a major role in the manning of the Indian army, Nepal was still closed to British travellers, and, indeed, remained so until after the end of the Raj in India in 1947.

The British refrained from making an overt attack on the place of Nepal in the Chinese world order. Nepal had its own system of diplomatic relations with Tibet when that region was totally closed to British influence. The British took no part in the Tibeto-Nepalese clash of 1854–56 or in the subsequent Tibeto-Nepalese agreement of 1856 which, under the cover of a general admission by both parties of some undefined dependence on China, provided for adjustment in the Tibeto-Nepalese boundary and for special Nepalese trading rights at Lhasa supervised by a Nepalese Resident in that city. The Ghurkas continued to send their quinquennial missions to Peking up to the end of the Manchu period, the last being in 1908, and the British made no protest. After the fall of the Manchus, British diplomatists in Peking from time to time denied the continuance of any special Chinese rights over Nepal, but there was no formal cancellation of the Manchu structure of Sino-Nepalese relations, which some officials of the new Chinese republic were wont to declare was still in force. After 1911, the rulers of Nepal on occasion informed the British Resident at Katmandu that the Sino-Nepalese tributary relationship, whatever its significance might have been, had lapsed with the end of the Manchu dynasty; yet, at the same time, members of the Rana family— the hereditary prime ministers of Nepal—were willing to appear in public wearing the robes and badges of Chinese official rank which the Manchus had conferred upon them.

In the Anglo-Nepalese Treaty of 1923, the Rana government acquired theoretical control over all its foreign relations. As far as the outside, non-Chinese, world was concerned, it continued up to 1947 to rely very much on British advice. To the north, however, the Nepalese maintained their own system of diplomatic contacts, which had been set up in the Manchu period. After 1912, of course, the problem of the precise nature of Nepalese relations with China became rather theoretical, since the Chinese ceased to have any control over territory in direct contact with Nepal. In 1951, with China's return to central Tibet, the problem revived. The Chinese had not forgotten their past suzerain status over Nepal; there exist publications of both the Kuomintang and the communists which make this clear enough. Had Nepal permitted itself to be involved in the great Sino-Indian boundary argument, it is likely that the Chinese would have started raising specific claims to rights over Nepalese territory.

When the British left the subcontinent in 1947, their Indian successors showed every sign of intending to cling to influence in Nepal. Indeed, they appear to have adopted a policy of active political intervention in Nepalese internal affairs with, as a possible ultimate objective, the union of Nepal with the Indian republic. While some Nepalese politicians favoured closer ties

K

with India, there can be no doubt that public opinion in the country was opposed to any diminution of Nepalese independence; and by the middle 1950s China was seen in Katmandu as an obvious counter to New Delhi. One factor in the overthrow of the Rana dynasty of hereditary prime ministers, which took place in this period, was the desire to resist Indian pressure.* The culmination of the policy of using China to balance India came in October 1961, when King Mahendra of Nepal signed in Peking a boundary treaty with the Chinese People's Republic, which amplified the Sino-Nepalese agreement of March 1960 on this question.

The Sino-Nepalese boundary passes for the greater part of its length through some of the world's most formidable mountains. Much of the terrain has been very inadequately surveyed, and it is clear that one of the major problems of boundary delimitation here has been the correlation between Nepalese and Chinese maps. As far as the author can make out by applying the verbal description in the 1961 agreement to 1:1,000,000 maps available to him, the agreed boundary follows almost precisely that shown during the period of the British Raj, with the exception of a small tract just to the east of Mount Everest (Jolo Lungma or Sagar Matha) where it would seem that a few square miles have passed from Nepal to China. But this apparent cession may imply no more than defective cartography.†

For two reasons we must consider the 1961 agreement as being generally favourable to Nepal. First: it carries with it a

---

* A palace revolution in 1950 overthrew the Ranas; and the monarchy, which for more than a century had been little more than a ceremonial institution, was restored to a position of power. In February 1951, this change was given formal recognition with the proclamation by King Tribhuvana of a constitutional monarchy.

† At one point during the Sino-Nepalese negotiations, the Chinese laid claim to much of the Everest massif south of the summit. In the final settlement, however, the boundary was made to pass through the summit, thus enabling both the Nepalese and the Chinese to look on Everest, the world's highest peak, as *their* mountain.

clear implication of China's abandonment of claims to some form of suzerainty over Nepal—claims which, as has been noted, the Kuomintang was inclined to adhere to. In the 1961 agreement and in the negotiations which preceded it, the Chinese People's Republic treated Nepal as a fully sovereign state. Second: all along the border between Nepal and Tibet, just as along the Middle Sector of the Sino-Indian border, there surely exist tracts where seasonal nomadism has created some conflict between Tibetan and Nepalese traditional jurisdictions. In the 1961 agreement, the Chinese appear to have made no effort to use such conflicts as the basis for territorial claims. No doubt transfrontier nomadism will continue to be an administrative problem, complicated perhaps by the hostility of some such nomad groups towards the Chinese communist regime in Tibet; but the delimitation of the border will certainly make these problems easier to solve.

The delimitation of the Sino-Nepalese border has been accompanied by the improvement of communications between Nepal and Tibet. By 1966, it became possible to travel by motor vehicle from Katmandu to Lhasa, thus giving the Nepalese an access, albeit long and difficult, to the outside world alternative to the route passing through Indian territory. This fact, alone, must make it easier for the Nepalese government to resist pressures from the south and to pursue a policy of neutrality. Nepal's situation in this respect makes it, in many ways, the very model of a neutral buffer state. Today it strikes a balance, not only between India and China, but also between China and the Soviet Union, and between both these communist powers and the United States. One pivot of this system of balance, there can be little doubt, is the stable Sino-Nepalese border.

BHUTAN

It is possible that Bhutan may turn out to be rather less successful than Nepal as a Sino-Indian buffer tract. Its population is predominantly Buddhist and more closely related in race and culture to the Tibetan plateau than to the Indian plains. The rulers of Bhutan certainly regarded themselves as in some way dependent upon the Tibetan regime of the Dalai Lama, at least until the coming of the Chinese communists; and in the nineteenth century there were occasions when Bhutanese chiefs accepted symbols of membership of the Chinese tributary system. The British, when they first came into contact with Bhutan in the late eighteenth century, considered the region to be in some way part of the Chinese sphere. In the early nineteenth century, they even explored the possibility of using Bhutanese mediation as a method of establishing those diplomatic contacts with Peking which were seen as a possible solution to the problems of British trade at Canton, and which were being frustrated by the established mechanism of Anglo-Chinese relations on the China coast.

From the outset, Anglo-Bhutanese relations were soured by crises along the line of demarcation between the Bhutanese hills and the plains of the Brahmaputra valley. The root of the problem lay in the claim of the Bhutanese hillmen to possession of the Duars: tracts forming a long strip of territory marking the transition from plains to hills.* The Bhutanese came down into the Duar tracts in the cold season; for the rest of the year, these territories were in the hands of plainsmen whom the Bhutanese came to regard as their tributaries. Conflict between Bhutan and the British-protected state of Cooch Behar over the ownership of Duar territory brought British intervention and the first Anglo-Bhutanese treaty, that of 1774. As British power expanded along the foothills of the Himalayas in Bengal and then, after the Burmese war of 1824–26, in Assam as well,

---

* Duar means 'gateway' and refers to the tracts where the mountain rivers of Bhutan debouch on to the plains of Bengal and Assam. There are, strictly speaking, eighteen Duars in all, eleven touching on Bengal and seven on Assam. The term Duars is now often used to cover the entire tract along the southern Bhutanese border.

so did friction over the Duar tracts increase. In 1841, the British annexed most of the Duar territory along the Assam-Bhutan border; a little later, in 1865, the Bengali Duars were permanently annexed, following a British campaign in the Bhutanese hills. The area removed from Bhutan by these transactions was a strip some 22 miles wide on the average and about 220 miles long. It has subsequently acquired a great economic importance as one of the major tea-growing areas of the subcontinent.

There can be no doubt that there are Bhutanese leaders who resent the loss of the Duars, and not only on economic grounds. Since the late nineteenth century, the Duars have provided a channel whereby new settlers, mainly of Nepalese origin, have penetrated into the southern districts of Bhutan. A similar process in Sikkim almost brought about the economic inundation of the Lepchas and other indigenous peoples of the state; and, from the end of the last century, the Bhutanese showed themselves to be most anxious lest the experiences of Sikkim be repeated in their country. Much of the history of Indo-Bhutanese relations in the latter part of the British period was concerned with problems arising from the movement of British Indian subjects across the border from the Duars into Bhutan proper.

Since 1865, when Anglo-Bhutanese contacts were regularised by the Sinchula Treaty, the southern border of Bhutan has been clearly defined. In the 1870s, the greater part of it was actually demarcated on the ground; the Bhutanese, ignoring for the moment any regrets about the Duars, do not contest its alignment. Of late, the main Bhutanese interest in the border with India is that it should be marked on Indian maps as an international boundary and not, as has often been the case, as an internal Indian administrative division. The Bhutanese have been endeavouring in such ways as this to indicate that they are a sovereign nation and not an Indian protectorate.

The international status of Bhutan is still not as clearly

defined as it might be. In 1865, the British established a protectorate of sorts over Bhutan, assuming responsibility for Bhutanese relations with the states of the subcontinent. No attempt was made at this time, however, to sever what the British considered to be ancient links with the Chinese and Tibetan worlds. The 1865 agreement made no mention of Sino-Bhutanese or Tibeto-Bhutanese relations; it seems to have assumed that these would continue in the way they always had. It was not until 1910, when the aggressive Central Asian policy of the last years of the Manchus seemed to threaten Bhutan, that a new Anglo-Bhutanese agreement was negotiated in which all Bhutanese foreign relations, including those with China and Tibet, were placed under the supervision of the Indian government. The 1910 treaty, however, did not provide for a British Resident in Bhutan or for any other means for the exercise of direct British influence in Bhutanese internal affairs. One result, there can be no doubt, was that the Bhutanese rulers continued to maintain close contacts with Lhasa where, from 1912 until 1950, the Chinese were not in a position of power.

With the Chinese reoccupation of Tibet in the 1950s, the status of Bhutan has once more become a question of more than academic interest. In 1949, the government of independent India signed a treaty with the Bhutanese which generally confirmed the provisions of the 1910 treaty. New Delhi, on this basis, considers it has the right to control Bhutanese foreign relations and to prevent Bhutan from taking such steps as applying for membership of the United Nations. Indian tutelage is much resented in some Bhutanese circles, and there can be no doubt that, since the eruption of the Sino-Indian crisis, there has been much thought given in Thimbu (the new Bhutanese capital) to an international posture along the lines of that adopted by Nepal. Only thus could the Bhutanese hope to come to a boundary agreement with China of the Nepalese type such as would settle apparent Chinese claims to more than 300 square miles of north-eastern Bhutan and end Chinese pretensions to suzerainty over the country.* To date, there seems to exist no comprehensive treaty defining the Sino-Bhutanese border, which is more than 200 miles in length.† The negotiations required for such a treaty, moreover, are unlikely to take place so long as New Delhi is able to maintain its present grip over Bhutanese external affairs.

At present Bhutan still performs a useful function as a buffer between China and India, but it does so less for political than geographical reasons. The internal communications of Bhutan effectively isolate the northern parts of the country from the Indian plains. However, since 1960, the Bhutanese, with Indian assistance, have embarked upon the building of roads and bridges on a scale which may well bring the physical presence of India here right up to the Chinese border, unless the Bhutanese can devise and execute a policy which combines an increase in Indian economic assistance with a decrease in Indian political influence. Bhutanese failure in this respect could well result in the country's being dragged into the morass of the Sino-Indian argument.

SIKKIM

The smallest of the Himalayan states, Sikkim has not been a buffer at all since the 1880s precisely because Indian influence extended right through it to its northern border. When the British first came into contact with the Himalayas, Sikkim was in far closer relations with Tibet than either Nepal or Bhutan was at that time. It could even be argued that Sikkim was under

* The precise nature of Chinese claims to Bhutanese territory is by no means clear. Recent Chinese maps showing Chinese claims to the Indian NEFA also appear to include within China a small portion of north-eastern Bhutan. There is no evidence, however, that the Chinese have ever raised formal and specific claims to this territory.

† There appear to have been Anglo-Bhutanese discussions of a rather informal nature over this border in 1918; but, of course, the Chinese took no part and neither did the Tibetans.

the rule of a Tibetan family and was a feudal dependency of the Dalai Lama's government at Lhasa. The British certainly considered this to be a fact. During the course of the Anglo-Nepalese war of 1814–16, the government of British India tried to use the Sikkimese ruling family as a channel of communication between Calcutta and the Chinese authorities in Lhasa, to whom it was considered expedient to explain British policy. Because of the connection with the north, the rate of British advance into Sikkimese territory during the nineteenth century was considerably slowed down. In 1835, the Indian government acquired Darjeeling and much of the Sikkimese foothill tracts, but the Anglo-Sikkimese war of 1860–61 did not result in British annexation right up to the Himalayan crests, even though the entire state was by treaty defined as being under British protection. No British Resident was at that time established at the Sikkimese capital, and no attempt was made to interfere with the traditional pattern of Tibeto-Sikkimese relations.

In 1886, however, the British found that they could not much longer delay a more permanent intervention in the internal affairs of Sikkim. In that year, the Indian government proposed to send a diplomatic mission to Tibet by way of Sikkim. The members of this party—the Colman Macaulay Mission—were provided with Chinese passports. The Tibetans, however, decided to oppose it, and for that purpose, apparently with the consent of the Sikkimese ruler, they set up military posts on Sikkimese territory astride the main road leading from India to Lhasa. In 1888, the British expelled the Tibetans after they had failed to get the Chinese to persuade their subjects to withdraw. Two years later, in 1890, the British negotiated a treaty with the Chinese which confirmed beyond all doubt British paramountcy in the state and defined verbally the Sikkim-Tibet border. At the same time, a British official was permanently stationed at Gangtok, the Sikkimese capital; thenceforward, the Indian government maintained a very considerable influence over the internal affairs of the state. This influence survived the transfer of power in 1947 and was reaffirmed in the agreement between India and Sikkim of 1950, in which New Delhi was confirmed in its responsibility for Sikkimese defence and foreign relations. With the development of the Sino-Indian crisis, India has stationed a formidable military force in Sikkim, making, in 1961, the gesture of allowing the Sikkimese to add to this force their own contingent of just under 300 men.

The Sikkim-Tibet border is the only stretch of the long Sino-Indian boundary which has been defined by a treaty signed by the Chinese. The alignment adopted in the 1890 Anglo-Chinese Convention, it should be noted, did not correspond precisely with the traditional border which, so the available evidence suggests, ran a few miles to the south of the watershed line in the extreme north of Sikkim and which, in Manchu times, had been marked out by pillars bearing tablets inscribed in both Chinese and Tibetan. The Tibetans greatly resented the definition of their border by negotiations in which they had not participated. When, in 1894, an attempt was made to demarcate on the ground the 1890 line by a joint Anglo-Chinese commission, the Tibetans reacted by secretly removing boundary markers. The result would seem to be that, by 1912, when the Chinese lost control of the Tibetan districts in territorial contact with Sikkim, demarcation of the 1890 boundary had not been achieved.

The Chinese communists have not contested the Anglo-Chinese Convention of 1890, even though they describe it as an 'unequal' treaty, and they accept the boundary line which it describes verbally. Modern Chinese writers, in both Kuomintang and communist times, have certainly made it clear that they look on Sikkim as having been detached from the Chinese world through imperialist pressure; but no Chinese government since 1890 has raised formal claims to sovereignty over Sikkim. It is perhaps of interest in this context to note that the Tibetans have raised such claims. In 1948, the Dalai Lama's government addressed a note to New Delhi which pointed out that the

British had now gone and enquired when former Tibetan territory would be restored to Lhasa. Sikkim, including the Darjeeling district, was one of the regions mentioned on this occasion.

The Sino-Indian argument over the Sikkim border which
broke out in 1963, and to which reference has already been
made in chapter 6, does not derive from a Chinese assertion of
past Tibetan claims to Sikkimese sovereignty. On the contrary,
it is the result of a Chinese argument to the effect that the
Indians have failed to respect the Sikkim-Tibet border as it was
defined by the Anglo-Chinese Convention of 1890. The main
significance of this particular problem is to be found less in
boundary alignment than in the fact of the direct contact of
intensively administered Chinese and Indian districts. Had
Sikkim managed to retain in the British period the buffer
properties of Nepal and Bhutan, then problems of this kind
would not have arisen. The circumstances leading to British
intervention in Sikkim in the 1880s, nineteenth-century British
commercial aspirations, Anglo-Russian rivalry in Asia, and so
on—such factors no longer have much relevance for modern
India and China. Yet their consequences still affect contemporary frontier policy.

★

There can be no doubt that the present Chinese regime is well
aware of the significance of the Himalayan states as buffers
between itself and the Indian republic. For this reason alone, it
would seem unlikely that the Chinese would attempt direct
intervention in the internal affairs of these states save as a
counter to Indian measures. Some observers have detected a
Chinese policy directed towards the creation of an even more
effective buffer: a confederation of Himalayan states that might
eventually be expanded to embrace, not only Nepal, Sikkim and
Bhutan, but also Ladakh, the tribal areas of the NEFA in the
Assam Himalayas and, even, Nagaland. Good geopolitical
arguments could be adduced in support of such a confederation,

but the practical problems involved in its creation would seem to be insuperable, at least through peaceful methods. Moreover, the evidence that the Chinese have really given serious thought to a project of this kind is far from satisfactory. It is hard to escape the conclusion that the British alone possessed the power and the freedom of manœuvre to have turned the whole Himalayan range into a continuous buffer between the Indian subcontinent and Chinese Central Asia. Had they forced the Dogras to relinquish Ladakh and restored it to the dynasty which had ruled it until Gulab Singh's conquest in the 1830s; had they left the Gurkhas after the war of 1814–16 in control of Kumaon and Garwhal; had they been able in the latter part of the nineteenth century to limit the expansion of their influence into Sikkim; and had they not felt called upon in 1914 to advance their border in Assam from the edge of the Brahmaputra valley to the crests of the Assam Himalayas—then indeed such a buffer might have emerged in the post-colonial era. With so many regions of established direct Sino-Indian territorial contact, however, the prospect of such a buffer can now be no more than an exercise in imagination.

8

Burma

The British swallowed Burma in three gulps. After the first
Anglo-Burmese war of 1824–26, the direct consequence of
Burmese expansion into the British frontier on the North-East,
the government of India took over the Burmese conquests in
Assam and annexed parts of Arakan and the coastal Tenasserim strip which marches with Siam southwards towards the
Isthmus of Kra. In 1852, the British took over Lower Burma,
that is to say, the delta and lower reaches of the Irrawaddy
valley. In 1886, Upper Burma, with its capital at Mandalay,
was brought into the British fold. The whole of Burma thus
acquired was treated as a major administrative subdivision of
the British Indian empire until 1937, when it became a separate
colonial territory. (See Map 22.) All of British Burma became
the independent Union of Burma in 1948. Since that date,
Burma has remained outside the Commonwealth and, today,
British influence there has virtually disappeared.

The British did something in Burma which all the king's men
could not do for Humpty Dumpty. Burma had a series of great
falls, each to a very considerable degree the product of the policy
of the ruling Burman dynasty. The state broke into fragments,

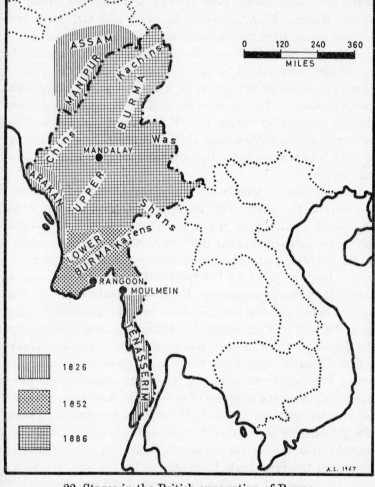

22. Stages in the British annexation of Burma.

but the British put it together again. Indeed, they did more: they gave Burma all sorts of bits and pieces which it is extremely unlikely it had ever held before with any firmness. The modern Burmese successors to the Konbaung dynasty inherited from the British a boundary embracing hill tracts on both sides of the Irrawaddy valley. Here lived non-Burman tribal groups: Shans, Karens, Kachins and Chins who, although they had without doubt from time to time acknowledged Burman over-lordship, yet established with the British relationships so much firmer and more precise as to be essentially different in kind. These relationships the Union of Burma acquired along with independence. It has been discovered in Rangoon, however, that it is easier to obtain title than vacant possession. The history of modern Burma has been dominated by a continuing conflict between the central government and the non-Burman hill people.

It is not easy to describe the traditional borders of a country like Burma. The power of the dominant groups in the plains has fluctuated greatly over the centuries. It reached an apogee during the great days of the Burman Konbaung dynasty which, in the middle of the eighteenth century, emerged victorious from a long struggle with the Mons and then embarked upon a career of territorial expansion. Repeated attacks were directed against Siam, and the Burmans took over the Tenasserim strip from the Gulf of Martaban to the Isthmus of Kra. Invasion by the forces of the Chinese Manchu dynasty was successfully resisted, greatly augmenting Burman influence over the Shans. In the late eighteenth and early nineteenth centuries, the Bur-mans undertook the conquest of territory to their west, advanc-ing into Manipur and Assam. In the process, however, they were also pressing on the eastern frontier of India and, in so doing, brought upon themselves the inevitable British counter-attack. Following the first Anglo-Burmese war of 1824–26, the Kon-baung dynasty lost its conquests in Assam and was deprived of Arakan and Tenasserim. In 1852, the dynasty, having failed to stabilise its relations with its British neighbours, was obliged to surrender Lower Burma (the region of the Irrawaddy delta); and in 1886, with the British annexation of Upper Burma (the Mandalay kingdom), the dynasty came to an end. It is an interesting, though academic, speculation to wonder how the frontiers of Burma would have evolved had the British contented themselves with the annexations of 1826 or 1852. What sort of boundary would the truncated Burmese state have established with a China which was, as the nineteenth century drew to its close, acquiring an increased sensitivity to frontier issues? The probability is that, without British resistance, the Chinese would have penetrated deep into what are today the Kachin and Karen states of the Union of Burma. It is hard to escape the conclusion that the boundaries of modern Burma—and their associated problems—are very much part of the imperial legacy.

The external boundaries of the Union of Burma can be divided into four sectors. First: there is the sector from Arakan to the Assam Himalayas which used to divide British Burma from British India. Since independence this boundary, in general well defined in the British period, has presented few problems. We have already commented on the East Pakistan-Burma boundary (see page 97). The main danger to the tranquillity of the India-Burma boundary derives, perhaps, from the Naga question. Nagas and other tribal groups discontented with Indian control straddle this boundary. Indian action in the Naga hills might in certain circumstances produce reactions on the Burmese side of the border. There is an analogy here with the Kurdish question. The Kurds occupy a frontier zone involving, not only Iraq, but also Iran and Turkey. The efforts of the Iraqi central government to put down Kurdish revolt, if extended into Iranian and Turkish territory, could not fail to have important international consequences. An Indian policy of striking at the sources of Naga supply across in Burma (including the alleged route from East Pakistan to Nagaland via the Chin hills) would surely give rise to an Indo-Burmese frontier crisis of some kind. Indophobia is endemic in Burma. At present, the risks of a clash are to some extent reduced by the fact that Rangoon has only a tenuous influence over the

Chin hills and neighbouring tracts. In other words, there is a buffer zone of sorts along this frontier.

The second sector of the Burmese boundaries marches with the extreme south-east corner of Chinese Tibet. Here the headwaters of the Irrawaddy are close to the upper valleys of the Salween, Mekong and Yangtze rivers. The region is sparsely populated, and it is improbable that significant pre-colonial Burman influence ever penetrated here. In 1914, the McMahon Line boundary between British India and Tibet was extended eastwards across the Taron (a tributary of the Nmaihka branch of the Irrawaddy) to provide a Sino-Burmese boundary. The Chinese did not accept this arrangement in 1914, but they did so implicitly in 1960. In theory, this particular alignment marks a Kachin-Tibetan ethnic divide; in fact, it represents a convenient line through a region so remote as to have been, until very recent times, a no-man's-land between Assam, Tibet, the upper Irrawaddy basin and Yunnan province in China.

The McMahon Line came to an end at the Isurazi pass on the Salween-Irrawaddy watershed. From the Isurazi pass to the Burma-Laos junction along the Mekong river, there is a long and complex boundary line between Burma and Yunnan, which evolved as a result of the British annexation of Upper Burma and the subsequent Anglo-French colonial competition. The Chinese in the colonial era treated this boundary with extreme suspicion, seeing it as a shield behind which the British would prepare for the extension of their influence into Yunnan. They considered that in places the line conflicted with established Chinese rights and interests. They felt that it was essentially a new boundary and not the traditional boundary of the pre-colonial Burmese state which, in any case, they regarded as a Chinese tributary.

Nearly half of the Sino-Burmese boundary which the Union of Burma inherited from the British had never been defined by Anglo-Chinese agreement. The Chinese, in British times, had not been prepared to accept the Salween-Irrawaddy divide as the legitimate border between Kachin state and Yunnan. They declared that Chinese territory embraced much of the upper reaches of the Irrawaddy basin, and as late as 1946 the Kuomintang was endeavouring to maintain a claim along these lines. Although in the British period much of the boundary between Yunnan and the Shan state had been settled with some measure of Chinese participation, the treaty basis for that settlement was seen in China as being extremely 'unequal'. Even the settlement of the disputed boundary in the Wa states sector, by League of Nations mediation in the 1930s and the Anglo-Chinese treaty of 1941, was still under active Kuomintang challenge on the eve of the Japanese attack on Pearl Harbor.

The Chinese communists inherited the Kuomintang's dislike of the treaty basis for the Sino-Burmese border. They further saw this border as one which posed an acute problem of frontier administration. Units of the defeated Kuomintang forces retreated into Burmese territory and showed every intention of remaining there as a threat, albeit a minor one, on the flank of the Chinese People's Republic. By 1953, the presence of Kuomintang troops in Burma had induced the Chinese communists to establish a number of 'defensive' posts across the border in violation of Burmese sovereignty: a situation which obliged the Burmese government to take active steps to secure the evacuation of the Kuomintang. With the assistance of the United Nations, Thailand and the United States, about half the Kuomintang troops were removed from Burma in 1954. This was seen in Rangoon as the essential preliminary step towards a Chinese communist withdrawal and a negotiation over the Sino-Burmese boundary such as would eliminate future crises. The course of negotiation was not easy, being marred by minor armed clashes between Chinese and Burmese patrols in remote frontier tracts. The final outcome, however, was the Sino-Burmese boundary agreement of October 1960 which defined the entire Sino-Burmese border, from the India-China-Burma

L

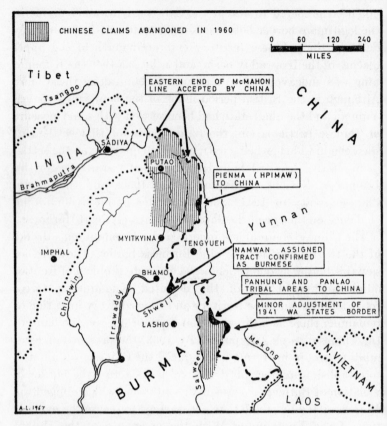

23. The Sino-Burmese boundary settlement of 1960.

trijunction in the Assam Himalayas to the Burma-China-Laos trijunction on the Mekong. (See Map 23.)

This Sino-Burmese boundary agreement of 1960 deserves to be studied in some detail, for it may well be an indication of the kind of border settlement the Chinese People's Republic would like to see all along its frontiers. The extreme north-western sector of the border, from its junction with India in the Assam Himalayas to the Isurazi pass on the eastern side of the

Taron river, forms part of the McMahon Line of 1914. This alignment, as has already been noted, the Chinese accepted without modification in 1960; but they did not do so because it *was* the McMahon Line. Nowhere in the 1960 Sino-Burmese agreement is there any mention of the proceedings of 1914. It is made clear that the boundary settled in 1960 was the result of discussions between a free China and a free Burma, acting in the spirit of the Five Principles of Peaceful Coexistence as proclaimed in the preamble to the Sino-Indian agreement on Tibet of 1954 and at the Bandung Conference of 1955. In fact, as a boundary between the remote tracts of northern Burma and eastern Tibet, the McMahon Line had much to recommend it, based as it was on careful survey and exploration during 1910–1913 in quest of a practicable Tibetan-Kachin ethnic divide.

To the south of the Isurazi pass, the old British demarcation of the Sino-Burmese border followed the line of the watershed between the Salween and Irrawaddy valleys for more than 100 miles before turning south-west towards Myitkyina on the upper Irrawaddy. Since the 1890s, China had actively contested this line, maintaining that in the past Chinese influence, cultural, economic and political, had penetrated into the Irrawaddy basin in the region generally known as the Triangle: a tract with one corner at Putao (Fort Hertz), just to the east of the divide between the Irrawaddy valley and the basin of the Brahmaputra in Assam. Between 1898 and 1912, there were a number of minor skirmishes between British and Chinese patrols in the Triangle, a major objective being control of the village of Hpimaw (or, as the Chinese called it, Pienma), just to the west of the Salween-Irrawaddy divide. The Chinese, though forced to withdraw, never abandoned their claims here. Following the defeat of Japan in 1945, they once more asserted claims to Burmese territory in the Triangle north of Myitkyina, reviving all the old arguments. The territory involved amounted to well over 10,000 square miles. Chinese claims were certainly greatly exaggerated, but some British officials concluded that, at least in respect to certain border villages along the Salween-Irrawaddy divide, they were not entirely without merit. In 1960, the Chinese abandoned the bulk of those claims to which the Manchus and the Kuomintang had adhered with such tenacity for more than half a century. Instead of tens of thousands of square miles, the Chinese were content with a modification of the old British border which gave them Hpimaw and two other villages, Gawlum and Kangfang—involving in all an area of 59 square miles.

South of the Triangle, and a few miles to the south-east of the Burmese frontier town of Bhamo, lay another district where there had been a degree of Sino-British dispute. This was the Namwan Assigned Tract: an area of less than 100 square miles which the British had acquired on 'perpetual lease' from China in 1897. The story of the acquisition of the Namwan Assigned Tract is typical of the process of frontier evolution during the height of Anglo-French competition in the 1890s. The problem lay in the definition of the limits of the British and French empires along the Mekong. The Kiang Hung district of the Shan state of Kengtung, which was under British control, extended to the east bank of the Mekong. In 1894, in an attempt to create some kind of buffer along the Mekong, the British ceded Kiang Hung to China on the explicit understanding that China would never cede it to any third power. In 1895, under considerable pressure, China ceded Kiang Hung to France. The British took this opportunity to revise drastically the 1894 agreement. In 1897, they not only informed China that the symbol of Burma's past dependence on China, the decennial tribute mission permitted by the Anglo-Chinese Convention of 1886, would be discontinued (no such mission had, in fact, ever been sent), but also that there would be a new adjustment of the Sino-Burmese border. A tract of territory, Namwan, where the Shweli joins the Salween, would be transferred to the British under perpetual lease, which meant that political control of the area would be for ever in British hands even though the tract was recognised as being in some vague way Chinese. The British further took this opportunity to annex a narrow strip along the east bank of the Salween in the region of Kunlong through which it was hoped the much discussed Burma-Yunnan railway would pass. This last tract received no special mention in the 1960 agreement which accepted Burmese sovereignty over it. In the case of the Namwan Assigned Tract, however, the Chinese ceded to Burma those residual rights admitted in the 1897 treaty. The area of the Namwan Assigned Tract was stated in 1960 to be some 85 square miles. In compensation for their abandonment of all claims to the Namwan Tract, the Chinese in 1960 were given a frontier district under the control of the Pan-hung and Panglao tribes. This tract, some 73 square miles in area, is located just to the south-west of Kunlong.

About half-way between the Namwan Assigned Tract and the Mekong lies the region of the Wa states: a tribal area which was brought under a measure of British influence in the 1890s. Some of the Wa tribes were head-hunters, and their territory was remote and ill-known. The border between the Wa states and the Chinese province of Yunnan was laid down originally by unilateral British action. In the early 1930s, it became the scene of active Anglo-Chinese competition, the main cause of which being the disputed ownership of silver mines. The Wa state boundary question in 1935 was submitted to a League of Nations Boundary Commission consisting of two British and two Chinese representatives, presided over by Colonel F. Iselin of Switzerland. The commission completed its work in 1937, and the result was formally accepted by the British and the Chinese in 1941. No sooner had the Kuomintang agreed to the Iselin award than it began to have second thoughts. After the defeat of Japan in 1945 it attempted to reopen the question of the Wa state boundary. However, in 1960 (though no specific mention was made of the fact), China confirmed the Iselin award in general but modified it in two details. The award had given

China the right to participate in certain mining ventures on the Burmese side; these rights the Chinese now renounced. The award had created in certain places a boundary which actually bisected villages; it was now agreed that where this was the case the boundary should, 'for convenience of administration', be so modified as to place the entire village concerned on either the Chinese or the Burmese side. By this arrangement two villages went to China and four villages to Burma.

In the Sino-Burmese boundary agreement of 1960, the Chinese communists accepted without modification the greater part of the British-created boundary to which the Kuomintang and the Manchus had been extremely reluctant to accord formal recognition. The small modifications that they did demand—in the Hpimaw region, in the exchange of residual Chinese rights in the Namwan Assigned Tracts for the Burmese cession of a portion of the Panhung and Panglao tribal areas, and in minor adjustments of the Wa states border—reveal the communist government of China as acting on principles which would not have been alien to a modern non-Chinese and non-communist state. Sweeping territorial claims were abandoned. In the Hpimaw region, China asserted claims based on past relationships: claims which some British officials in the early twentieth century did not feel they could dismiss out of hand. In the Namwan Assigned Tract, the Chinese surrendered undoubted rights of residual sovereignty for which they received territorial compensation. In the Wa states sector, they accepted the result of past international arbitration, with very minor modifications based on considerations of local frontier administration. All this produced an actual increase in Chinese territory of about 50 square miles—considerably less than Iran gained from Pakistan along the Baluchistan border as a result of negotiations which were completed at about the same time as the Sino-Burmese boundary agreement of October 1960.

It is hard to escape the conclusion that, in the 1960 agreement with Burma, the Chinese were not seeking Burmese territory.

Their main interest was in the securing of a stable defined boundary. Where they felt that they possessed good traditional rights, as in the case of Hpimaw, they insisted on some modification of the old British boundary. Elsewhere, however, they were prepared to abandon extensive territorial claims which neither the Manchus nor the Kuomintang had been willing to give up. It seems likely that the departure of the British has altered profoundly the strategic nature, in Chinese eyes, of the Sino-Burmese border. The contemporary Chinese diplomatists, in effect, have adopted a modern version of the traditional policy of their predecessors in the pre-colonial era. Burma has become a kind of Chinese 'protectorate' in the sense that it has adopted a 'neutral' foreign policy—that is to say, a policy of exclusion from its soil of potential or actual anti-Chinese influences. This has been achieved by diplomacy and not by territorial conquest. So long as Burma remains 'neutral', it seems likely that the Sino-Burmese border will remain stable.

The final sector of the Burmese boundary, stretching from the Mekong to Point Victoria on the western shore of the Isthmus of Kra, separates Burma from Laos and Thailand. This line cuts through a region where, in pre-colonial times, the Burmese competed actively with the Thais. It was Anglo-French influence which brought stability here, establishing the Burma-Laos border along the Mekong, and defining the Burma-Thailand boundary during the last years of the nineteenth century. This line is not seriously challenged today, yet it is in some respects an artificial boundary with elements of instability. The Thais are related ethnically and linguistically to the Shans. There have long been close connections between northern Thai districts like Chiengmai and Shan states like Kengtung. During the Second World War, the Japanese actually transferred some Shan tracts to Thai administration. Farther south, also, this boundary poses ethnic problems. There are Karen tribes on both sides of it. In the Thai-Malay peninsula, the line cuts through Mon populations which, until the middle of the eighteenth century, had all experienced a long history of subordination to Thai dynasties.

The nature of the Burma-Thailand border suggests the possibility of crises in certain hypothetical situations. First: any serious decline of the power of the Burmese central government —especially if it were to occur in a period of active anti-Chinese American influence in mainland South-east Asia—might well tempt the authorities in Bangkok to give thought to territorial expansion in that westward direction which had once been blocked by European imperial frontier policy. Second, and on a more immediately local level: there is some evidence that opponents of General Ne Win's military regime in Burma have gathered in the Kwai valley on the Thai side of the border. So long as they remain there, there will always be the danger of frontier incidents arising from the activities of these Burmese refugee groups.

9

Thailand

By the end of the eleventh century AD, the Thais—an ethnic group cognate to the Chinese and closely related to the Shans and the Laos—had begun to migrate from their homeland in what is now the Kweichow, Kwangsi and Yunnan provinces of China towards the basin of the Menam (Chao Phraya) and the north-west frontier of the Khmer empire.* By the end of the thirteenth century, a powerful Thai state had arisen which was based on the city of Sukhotai on the middle reaches of the Menam valley. It enjoyed close relations with the Mongol (Yuan) dynasty then ruling China, and its southward expansion took place at the expense of the declining Khmer empire. In 1350, the centre of Thai power was moved farther down the Menam to Ayuthia. Almost a century later, in 1431, the Thais captured and sacked Angkor, obliging the Khmers to move their capital to Phnom Penh, which has remained ever since the centre of Cambodian national identity.

By no stretch of imagination can it be maintained that the

---

* There are about 10 million people in China today who speak languages closely related to Thai,

present boundaries of Thailand coincide with those of the Thai kingdom of Ayuthia as it was founded in the middle of the fourteenth century. The Thai domination of the Menam valley gave rise to an extremely complicated and turbulent history of political evolution, involving both external and internal conflict. Many are the themes in this story: the struggle between Ayuthia and the Thai kingdom of Chiengmai; Thai competition with the Laos for the domination of the Mekong valley; the expansion of Thai control and influence down the peninsula towards the Malay world south of the Isthmus of Kra; the struggle with the Burmans during the course of which, in the eighteenth century, the Thai state was almost anihilated; and, finally, the competition between the Thais and the Viets to their east over the remnants of Khmer empire in Cambodia.

The year 1767 marks the nadir of modern Thai history, for in that year the Burmans captured and destroyed the Thai capital at Ayuthia. Thereafter followed a period of recovery during which the present Thai kingdom, based on Bangkok near the mouth of the Menam, was born. The Burmans were repelled and Thai dominion was restored in Chiengmai. The Thais re-established their power in the peninsula, though Burma retained hold of the Tenasserim strip. The Lao kingdoms of the Mekong valley were brought under Bangkok's suzerainty and Thai influence once more thrust deep into the western districts of Cambodia. A foreign observer in the middle of the nineteenth century could not escape the conclusion that the energetic rulers of the Bangkok dynasty had turned Thailand into an expanding state. In the second half of the century, however, its expansion was abruptly checked by the formation of British Burma and Malaya, and of French Indochina: a process which nearly brought about the obliteration of Thailand as an independent state.

The Thais, however, managed to survive the flood-tide of European conquest in Asia without submitting to colonial rule. This was a remarkable feat of which all Thais are justly proud.

In part, it was due to the skill and flexibility of Thai diplomatists and statesmen who, unlike their Burmese and Vietnamese
neighbours, were adept in the art of timely compromise.
But the suavity of Thai princes would probably have been
of little avail had their country not occupied a buffer position
between the British and French empires. There are good
grounds for supposing that only the desire to minimise the area
of direct imperial contact prevented the evolution of an Anglo-
French boundary down the Menam. Moreover, though Thailand
was not colonised, Bangkok nevertheless had to accept colonial
dictation as to the alignment of boundaries; and, in the process,
it was obliged to give up large tracts of territory which Thais
felt were or ought to be theirs. (See Map 24.)

The land boundaries of modern Thailand can be divided into
four main sectors, each with its own history and problems.
First: there is the long Burma-Thailand border running southward from the Mekong to Victoria Point in the Isthmus of Kra.
Second: there is the Laos-Thailand boundary in the Mekong
valley. Third: there is the Thailand-Cambodia border, which
extends from the Mekong to the Gulf of Siam. Finally: there is
the border between Thailand and Malaya which runs from the
South China Sea to the Indian Ocean across the Malay peninsula.

The border between Burma and Thailand—the scene of
almost continual conflict between Burman and Thai dynasties
since the sixteenth century—was finally stabilised in the nineteenth century as a result of the British annexations in Burma.
In 1826, following the first Anglo-Burmese war, the British
annexed the Tenasserim strip from the Gulf of Martaban to the
Isthmus of Kra. Inhabited mainly by Mons, this region traditionally had been under some kind of Siamese suzerainty, and
had come under Burmese rule solely by virtue of military conquest on the part of the Konbaung dynasty. The British considered handing Tenasserim back to the Thais, and no doubt
they might have done so had King Rama III's government

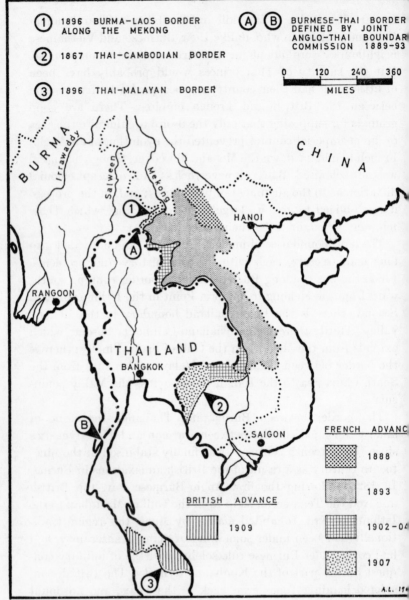

24. British and French definitions of the boundaries of Thailand.

been a bit more forthcoming in its negotiations in 1826 with the ambassador of the East India Company, Captain Henry Burney. Having decided against its return to Siamese control, the British then considered placing Tenasserim under the rule of an indigenous Mon dynasty; but descendants of the old Mon royal family could not be found either in Tenasserim or among the Mon refugees living in Siam. Outright British annexation, in these circumstances, appeared to be the only practicable solution to the problem of Tenasserim.

Looking backward from the present to 1826, one can now see that a number of quite different histories were possible for the Tenasserim strip. Had a Mon dynasty been restored, the region might have survived into the post-colonial era as a state in its own right, adding yet one more element to the political map of modern mainland South-east Asia. Had it come under the control of Bangkok, modern Thailand would have touched the Indian Ocean at the Gulf of Martaban. Had Tenasserim been placed under an indigenous dynasty enjoying British protection, and had at the same time British contact with the Malay peninsula been centred on Phuket island (Junk Ceylon), as Francis Light had first proposed, rather than on Penang island much farther to the south, then it is possible that British Malaya would have swallowed all southern Thailand, in the process digesting the whole area from the isthmus to Moulmein. There can be little doubt that the major factor in the Burmese retention of Tenasserim lay in British colonial policy and its consequences. The story of Tenasserim provides an admirable example, from the non-colonial point of view, of the almost accidental process of Asian boundary evolution in the colonial era.

The 1826 boundary between British Burma and Thailand followed the crest of the Bilauktaung and Dawna ranges from Victoria Point to the pass just east of Mae Sot on the old trade route from Sukhotai to the Gulf of Martaban. This boundary was extended northwards by the British annexation of Lower

Burma in 1852, for some of its way following the *thalweg* of the Salween river. After the annexation of Upper Burma in 1886, the final stretch of this border—from the Salween to the Mekong —was created. This sector first cut through regions inhabited by Karens and then, farther north, divided the Shan states from Chiengmai: a city with which many Shan groups had in the past possessed close political and cultural relations. It is unlikely that the Thai rulers ever had any particular interest in the Karens. The Shans, however, were certainly seen in Bangkok as being actual or potential members of the Thai world order; had the British not annexed Upper Burma, it is reasonable to suppose that the last decade of the nineteenth century would have produced a forward Thai policy in the Shan states comparable with that which King Chulalongkorn was endeavouring to execute in Laos on the eve of the French annexation.

The boundary between Thailand and the Shan states in British Burma was decided in outline by the Anglo-Siamese Commission of 1889–90 which was headed by Ney Elias, a British official with great experience of frontier matters, and which had as one of its members the energetic J. G. Scott who was shortly to play such a prominent part in the evolution of the Burma-Yunnan border. The Siamese participation in the commission was slight, to say the least. By 1893, most of the practical details of the new boundary had been worked out, and in the process a number of tributary relationships between Shan chiefs (*sawbwas*) and Bangkok were effectively terminated.

It can be argued that Thailand lost much by the evolution of the Shan states' boundary. The Japanese certainly saw this point, and in 1943 as part of their general readjustment of Siamese borders they 'restored' to Thailand the Shan states of Kengtung and Mongpan. These, of course, reverted to Burma in 1945, but there are certainly politicians in Bangkok today who feel that they should still be Thai. In fact, however, the Thai control over these Shan districts was in the late nineteenth century indirect and remote to say the least. Their loss was theoretical rather than practical, and in exchange for it the government in Bangkok gained a stable border with Burma which, for the first time in centuries, was free from the danger of Burmese military incursions. Once the Anglo-French colonial balance in mainland South-east Asia was completed in 1909, the Thais had a secure western flank.

Just as the British annexations in Burma created the modern Burma-Thailand boundary, so did French colonial policy produce the present Laos-Thailand boundary. The frontier history of Laos will be considered in greater detail in chapter 10; it suffices here to note that, during the course of the nineteenth century, the Bangkok dynasty had established a suzerainty of sorts over most of the states to the east of the Mekong which today make up the kingdom of Laos. In the 1880s, when it became obvious that the French intended to expand up the Mekong from their Vietnamese possessions, the Thais initiated a policy of active intervention in Laotian affairs. A war between France and Thailand nearly resulted, in which Thai independence would have been severely limited if it survived at all. In the event, however, and to a great extent because of the British factor in the diplomatic equation, the Thais came to terms with the French in 1893. The Laotian states along the east bank of the Mekong were brought under French rule and the eastern boundary of Thailand from Burma to Cambodia was defined by the course of the Mekong. This line was subsequently modified to the disadvantage of the Thais. In 1904, the French acquired the Sayaboury tract to the west of the Mekong opposite Luang Prabang; at the same time they also removed from Thai control a fragment of the old kingdom of Champassak on the west bank of the Mekong.

In late 1940, following the German occupation of France and the establishment of Japanese control over the pro-Vichy regime in Indochina, the Thais waged what is sometimes referred to as the Franco-Thai war. One Thai objective was the recovery of Laotian tracts on the west bank of the Mekong;

25. Territory 'restored' to Thailand by Japan, 1941–45.

another lay in territorial acquisition in Cambodia. The war was, in fact, a charade: a device whereby the Japanese, the real masters in Indochina, could transfer French territory to the Thais. Through Japanese 'mediation', the Franco-Thai treaty of Tokyo was signed on May 9, 1941, whereby Thailand gained the two trans-Mekong tracts of Laos, and also the Cambodian territory to which further reference will be made in the next chapter. The Tokyo arrangements of 1941 were reversed following the Japanese surrender in 1945. (See Map 25.)

The process of history which resulted in the evolution of the modern Thailand-Laos boundary has produced two major problems which still affect the policy of Bangkok. First: the ruling Thai oligarchy has not entirely abandoned its desire to possess influence over the internal affairs of Laos. The right-wing faction in modern Laotian politics has sometimes assumed the appearance of being, as it were, the Vientiane branch of the Bangkok government. The maintenance of a friendly regime along the east bank of the Mekong is clearly of strategic importance to Thailand; and there can be no doubt that American interest in Laos is very much conditioned by American interest in Thailand, the staunchest ally of the United States on the South-east Asian mainland. The inherent political instability of Laos—largely the product of the fact that this state emerged into the post-colonial era as the somewhat artificial creation of the French—makes it unlikely that a purely Laotian solution of its own internal problems will seem to meet Thai security requirements. This is all the more so because of the second problem inherent in the present alignment of the Thailand-Laos border: namely, that it leaves significant Lao populations on the Thai side. These minority groups are situated in north-eastern Thailand in a region, far from Bangkok, which has benefited but little from the rapid economic development that has been taking place in the Menam valley and the peninsula. Discontent in the north-east, particularly if exploited or encouraged from the east bank of the Mekong, could well present the Bangkok authorities with serious military problems. The situation in north-eastern Thailand, combined with more general strategic arguments, might conceivably induce Bangkok to conclude that Thailand would be safer and happier if its boundary enclosed territory on the east bank of the Mekong—coinciding, in other

M

words, with the idea of Thai territorial limits which King Chulalongkorn held in the late nineteenth century.

A third sector of the external boundaries of Thailand runs
from Laos to the Gulf of Siam and separates Thai from Cambodian territory. This sector, like the Thailand-Laos boundary,
emerged as the outcome of French imperial policy, checked to
some degree by the countervailing force of the British presence
in Burma and Malaya. In the middle of the nineteenth century,
the Cambodian kingdom—successor to the great empire of the
Khmers who built Angkor—was on the point of being squeezed
out of existence by the combined pressures of the Thais and the
Vietnamese. The French intervention in Annam in 1858–59
led inevitably to a French intervention in Cambodia, which
became in the 1860s a French protectorate. The outcome was
the definition of the Thai-Cambodian boundary by a series of
Franco-Thai agreements. The first of these, in 1867, left Thailand in possession of the western Cambodian province of Siem
Reap (in which are situated the Angkor sites) and Battembang.
In 1904–7, however, the Thais were obliged to give up Siem
Reap and Battembang and to accept a boundary line which, for
some of its length, ran along the watershed of the Dangrek hills
separating the Cambodian plain from the Korat plateau.

The Thais have never been content with this settlement. In
1941, they were in no way reluctant to accept Japanese mediation in securing Siem Reap and Battembang from the Vichy
French authorities in Indochina. In December 1946, more than
a year after the Japanese surrender, the Thais formally returned
the two provinces to a Cambodia which, by that time, had
reverted to French control; but Siem Reap and Battembang
appear still to be engraved on many Thai hearts. Since Cambodia gained its independence from France in 1954, relations
between Bangkok and Phnom Penh have for long periods been
extremely tense. A consequence of this has been the development of two boundary disputes: one concerned with the ancient
Khmer temple of Preah Vihear on the Dangrek watershed (and

which probably symbolises in Thai minds the loss of the Khmer monuments at Angkor in Siem Reap province); and the other with the precise location of a sector of the boundary between the Dangrek hills and the Gulf of Siam. The Preah Vihear dispute was submitted to the International Court of Justice at The Hague, which in 1962 awarded the temple to Cambodia. All Thais, and a minority of the judges on the International Court, consider this to be a miscarriage of justice.* The second dispute, which concerns the stretch of boundary east of the Thai town of Chantaburi, has been very much kept alive by the Thais who continually allege Cambodian aggressions and outrages here. There can be little doubt that, in any repartition of

* The essence of the Preah Vihear problem lies in a conflict between the verbal definition of the Thai-Cambodian boundary as it was stated in the Franco-Siamese treaty of 1904 and the alignment of that boundary on a French map of 1907. According to the 1904 treaty, the Thai-Cambodian boundary should follow the main waterparting line of the Dangrek Range separating the Korat Plateau in Thailand from the Cambodian plains. The 1907 map appeared to indicate that the boundary should depart from the waterparting line so as to place the Preah Vihear temple, an ancient Khmer monument, on the Cambodian (French) side. This boundary the Thais, by their failure to protest against it, were deemed to have accepted. During the pleadings before the International Court of Justice, it proved extremely difficult to establish exactly where the line of the waterparting lay; the balance of the evidence suggested that it actually passed through the centre of the disputed temple. The Court, in these circumstances, decided to hold to the boundary on the 1907 map (which it was argued the Thais had accepted by default) rather than to endeavour to lay out on the ground the verbal definition of the 1904 treaty. The Court was by no means unanimous in this decision, and there were minority opinions in favour of Thailand. Since receiving the Court's decision, the Thais have, in effect, demarcated unilaterally the boundary in the Preah Vihear region by the erection of a high fence. It must be admitted, however, that the main Thai objective was less the desire for boundary demarcation than the wish to spite the Cambodians: the Thai fence spoils the view from the temple. It has been reported that, for a brief period in 1966, a Thai patrol reoccupied Preah Vihear, only to depart with an exchange of fire after the arrival of a Cambodian detachment.

mainland South-east Asia—such as one imagines could possibly
emerge from an extreme development of the crisis in Vietnam
(the overthrow of the present Cambodian regime, for example)
—the Thais would expect to get portions at least of Siem Reap
and Battembang provinces, including the Preah Vihear temple.

The fourth and final sector of the Thai boundary separates
Thailand from Malaya. In the first half of the nineteenth
century, the Bangkok dynasty considered the entire Malay
peninsula to fall within its sphere of influence. In the north of
the peninsula, the Thai influence, though intermittently exercised, was real enough; in the south, it was tenuous indeed. Into
this sphere the British began to penetrate in the late eighteenth
century, when the East India Company acquired the island of
Penang from the sultan of Kedah, a dependant of the Bangkok
dynasty. In 1909, the British advance came to a halt with the
transfer from Thailand to British Malaya of the states of Kedah,
Perlis, Kelantan and Trengganu. The resultant boundary was
well enough defined, and in recent years disputes concerning it
have usually been confined to the claims and counter-claims,
discussed by local officials, arising from the tendency of the
owners of rubber estates to move boundary markers a few feet
one way or another.

The Thai-Malay boundary, however, does contain within it
elements of instability which could easily exert their influence
in the event of a major change in the political climate in Bangkok or Kuala Lumpur. First: the 1909 boundary settlement did
not complete the process of integrating all the Malay states of
the peninsular within British Malaya. A group of Malay states
in the Patani-Singora region, which had close dynastic ties with
British Malaya, remained in Thailand.* A vehemently racist
Malay party could well raise irredentist arguments which would
greatly strain Malayan-Thai relations. Second: as the Japanese

* One authority gives the Malay population of southern Thailand as
750,000 (1962 estimate). This equals about one-fifth of the Malay
population of Malaya.

invasion in 1941 demonstrated beyond all doubt, Malaya is extremely vulnerable to attack from the direction of the Kra Isthmus. The 1909 boundary did not help the British in 1941 in their attempts to oppose a Japanese invasion by way of Singora. Just north of the 1909 boundary, the remnants of the Malayan communist rebellion, led by Chin Peng, to this day maintain themselves in jungle concealment. They pose no real threat at present, but with active Thai support they could be very dangerous indeed. A neutralist, that is to say Chinese-oriented, Thailand might not feel itself called upon to oppose the extension of Chinese communist influence in Malaya; it might, indeed, attempt to purchase its own independence through assistance to the Chinese elsewhere. One must not forget the object lesson of Thai diplomacy in 1941–45. In 1945, the British gave serious thought to the strengthening of the Malayan land frontier by a northward advance of the boundary. They were frustrated, so it is generally accepted, by American pressure. In certain conditions (those following on an American débâcle in Vietnam, for example, unlikely though such an event might seem), the independent Malayan authorities could well revive British strategic thinking.

One could also imagine certain circumstances in which the Thais would look for territorial acquisition at the expense of Malaya: for example, if Malaya fell to Chinese communists while Thailand remained under an American defensive umbrella. In 1943, the Japanese undid the territorial transfer of 1909 and restored Kelantan, Trengganu, Perlis and Kedah to nominal Thai sovereignty. There are a number of prominent Malayan politicians and officials who served for a while the Thai-Japanese regime in northern Malaya. Japan's defeat in 1945 automatically brought the four northern Malay states back under British rule, and they now are firmly within independent Malaysia. It is not difficult, however, to find Thais who will speak with regret of these 'lost' Malayan territories.

Indochina:
Laos, Cambodia and Vietnam

The French empire in Indochina occupied an area of about 255,000 square miles. It was a little bit bigger than metropolitan France and somewhat smaller than Burma. It could hardly compare in area with the 1,500,000 square miles of British India. Despite its modest size, however, French Indochina contained much diversity. It represented no one traditional entity. Vietnam, Laos and Cambodia, while they had long been in contact with each other, had never before been united into a single state. Their union under the French was not to be continued in the age of Asian independence. In 1954, French Indochina broke up *de facto* into four states: North Vietnam, South Vietnam, Laos and Cambodia—though, in theory, the division between the two Vietnams was intended to be only temporary. Since then, the process of fragmentation has continued in Laos which, by 1966, had become the sphere of at least two distinct sovereignties. (See Map 26.)

The French expansion into Vietnam towards the frontiers of the metropolitan Chinese provinces of Kwangsi and Yunnan provoked a far more violent Chinese reaction than did the

26. French Indochina.

British advance into Upper Burma. Although the Peking authorities acquiesced in the French conquests in the southern portions of Vietnam, they were not prepared to let the French take over Tonkin without a fight. Vietnam had long formed part of the world of Chinese diplomacy. The emperor of Annam sent a tribute mission to Peking once every three years, while Tonkin was a frontier zone of the Chinese state which in past periods had been under direct Chinese administration. When the French, in 1882, launched what they intended to be the final drive to bring Tonkin under their control, China actively intervened. The result was the Franco-Chinese war of 1885 in which the French did not have everything their own way. The Chinese, of course, could not match the French navy which was able to dominate Formosa and the Pescadores and to destroy a Chinese fleet in Foochow harbour. In Tonkin, however, Chinese land forces in March 1885 inflicted a defeat on the French at Langson near the Kwangsi border. The Langson crisis, while militarily of relatively minor significance, had the most profound political consequences in Paris, where the Indochinese venture was far from popular. Clemenceau, who considered that France in its quest for overseas colonies was being diverted from its true objective—the expulsion of Germany from Alsace and Lorraine—used the reports of Langson to bring about the parliamentary defeat of the cabinet of Jules Ferry. Clemenceau, in the process, produced an equation between French colonial expansion and collaboration with Germany which it was not easy to dispel. The defeat of Ferry—the great advocate of French colonial expansion—was accompanied by public cries of 'Ferry Tonkin, Ferry Bismarck', and it was almost immediately followed by the Franco-Chinese Treaty of Tientsin of June 1885. In some ways, the Tientsin agreement was one of the least 'unequal' treaties which China had to make with the Western powers in the latter part of the nineteenth century, since it was negotiated from a position of some Chinese strength. It settled the status of Tonkin, where the Chinese could not avoid acknowledging French rule, and provided for a definition by joint boundary commission of the border between the French acquisitions in Tonkin and the Chinese provinces of Kwangsi, Kwangtung and Yunnan.

In 1887, a Franco-Chinese agreement on the Tonkin boundary was signed in Peking. It defined verbally a line from the Gulf of Tonkin to the Black river. In 1895, following the French annexations in Laos, the 1887 boundary was modified slightly and extended westwards to the Mekong, the *thalweg* of which in 1896 was accepted by Anglo-French agreement as marking the boundary between French Laos and British Burma. The boundary system created in 1887–95 has, on the whole, stood the test of time, and the present Chinese regime would seem to challenge neither its alignment nor its treaty basis.* There were, of course, French colonial officials who hoped for further French expansion into Yunnan and Kwangsi; but their ambitions, lacking the support of Paris, did not produce boundary changes. The French imperial legacy in Indochina does not involve doubt as to the whereabouts of the line of demarcation between Tonkin and Laos on the one hand and China on the other. The French, however, did leave behind them major problems concerning the political nature and the internal and non-Chinese boundaries of the successor states to their Indochinese empire.

LAOS

Laos is probably the oddest, if also the most charming, example of the consequences of European imperial policy in Asia. The

---

* The Chinese could, it is worth noting, raise claims to tracts in the extreme north-west of Laos which had been recognised as being Chinese in the Anglo-Chinese Convention of 1894 and which China then ceded to France in the boundary agreement of 1895. It is interesting that the communist regime in Peking does not appear to have raised this point. No doubt it would give rise to some discussion were there ever to be a Sino-Laotian boundary agreement on the pattern of the Sino-Burmese boundary agreement of 1960.

Lao people, closely related in both race and culture to the Thais,
occupy the middle reaches of the Mekong valley. For more than
four centuries, their history has been one of resistance to pressure from Burma, Thailand, Vietnam and (though for geographical reasons to a rather lesser extent) from China as well.
The last powerful Lao state of the pre-colonial period, the kingdom of Lan Chang, broke up in the early eighteenth century.
By the middle of the nineteenth century, what is today Laos
was fragmented into a number of petty principalities of which
Luang Prabang, Vientiane, Champassak and Xieng Khouang
were the most important. Luang Prabang, Vientiane and Champassak were under varying degrees of Thai influence. Xieng
Khouang trod an uneasy path between the Thais and the
Vietnamese.

These states were dominated by the Lao people, sedentary
cultivators of wet-rice who occupy the alluvial plains of the
Mekong basin. Some of the upper valleys of the Mekong system,
particularly in the north near the borders of Yunnan and
Tonkin, are inhabited by Thai tribal groups, related to but
distinct from the Lao: fragments left behind in the flood of Thai
migration from Yunnan into the South-east Asian mainland.
Like the Lao, most of the Thai tribes cultivate wet-rice. Another
group in the Laotian hills, rarely living below 3,000 feet and
practising slash-and-burn agriculture, are the Meo (or Miao)
and the Man (or Yao) tribes: people with some degree of affinity
with the Yunnanese and who appear to have moved down from
western China in a continuing process of migration since the
1850s to occupy the same kind of terrain as the Kha (a Laotian
word meaning slave) who are the aboriginal, pre-Lao, inhabitants of the region. Some Kha groups show Negrito racial
characteristics, and others appear to be members of the Mon-
Khmer linguistic family. Like the Meo or the Man, the Kha live
in the hills, and their agriculture is mainly of the slash-and-burn
pattern. Where they have come into contact with the people of
the valleys, Lao or Thai, they have generally been enslaved or

exploited. In 1921, the Lao made up 52 per cent of the population of French Laos, the Thai tribes 15 per cent, the Meo and the Man 3 per cent and the Kha groups 27 per cent. While the Lao and the Thai together provided the overwhelming bulk of the population, the Kha and other hill tribes certainly occupied the greater part of the area; and Lao influence in many Kha districts must, in the pre-colonial period, have been slight to say the least.

In the 1860s and 1870s, the Manchus lost control of large tracts of western China as a result of rebellion by Muslim and other tribal populations. One consequence was the emergence of Chinese bandit groups—always a feature of turbulent epochs in Chinese history—some of whom moved south from Yunnan into Laos and Tonkin. The Ho, as these bandits were known locally, threatened to devastate the Lao states of Luang Prabang and Vientiane, which in desperation sought the active protection of the Bangkok dynasty. The Thais, however, were unable to restore order on the east bank of the Mekong by the time that the French had completed their annexation of Tonkin in 1885. Faced with a disturbed north-west frontier in Tonkin, and attracted by the prospect of control over the Mekong (which appeared to provide a potential trade route into the heart of western China*), the French also decided to intervene in Laos against the Ho bands. They found their justification in the fact that many of the Lao and Thai states had possessed dependent relationships, not only with Bangkok, but also with the Annamese dynasty at Hue. Exploiting these relationships, the French in 1888 annexed the Sipsong Chu Thai: the Thai tribal area to the east of Tonkin in which is situated the town of

---

* Some of the pioneers of French rule in Indochina, like Francis Garnier, saw the Mekong as an artery of commerce comparable with the Yangtze. Up the Mekong, they believed, French trade would find its way deep into the heartland of the Chinese empire. In fact, however, it turned out that rapids made the Mekong an extremely difficult waterway.

Dienbienphu, where French colonialism in Asia was to meet its
final defeat in 1954. By 1893, the French had gone much
farther, still exploiting ancient relationships between the Lao
states and the empire of Annam which they claimed to have
inherited. They obliged the Thais to retreat, taking over all of
what is today Laos up to the east bank of the Mekong. In 1904,
they added to their Laotian possessions the Sayaboury and
Champassak tracts on the west bank of the Mekong.

The Sipsong Chu Thai—the district of the twelve Thai tribes,
which the French annexed in 1888—was formally incorporated
into the French protectorate of Tonkin in 1895, thus trans-
ferring to what is today North Vietnam a tract over which both
Laos and Thailand could claim that they possessed traditional
suzerain rights. The rest of the French acquisitions in what is
today Laos were organised, with a few minor adjustments (like
the transfer of the town of Stung Treng to Cambodia), into the
French territory of Laos under the control of a Chief Resident
at Vientiane. Of the old Lao states, Champassak, Vientiane and
Xieng Khouang were annexed outright by France and became
its colonies. Luang Prabang, however, managed to survive
under its own dynasty as a French protectorate.

During the Second World War, the Japanese put into execution a policy for the creation of a united Laotian state under the
rule of the Luang Prabang dynasty. This took place in two
stages. First: in 1941, the Vichy French authorities, who in
Indochina were collaborating actively with the Japanese, made
over Vientiane and Xieng Khouang to King Sisavangvong of
Luang Prabang. Second: in March 1945, following the Japanese
assumption of direct control in Indochina, King Sisavangvong
was urged by the Japanese to declare the whole of Laos independent of France under his leadership. The king was reluctant to
do this and, by the time of the Japanese surrender, he had only
brought himself to the point of declaring independence for those
territories covered by the 1941 treaty, which excluded such
southern districts as Champassak. Laos under the Japanese, it

should also be noted, excluded those tracts on the western bank of the Mekong which the French had taken from the Thais in 1904. These were restored to Thailand in 1941 as one result of the so called Franco-Thai war.

After the Japanese surrender and the restoration of French control, the process of converting the Luang Prabang dynasty into the monarchy of all Laos continued. As a constitutional monarchy with its royal capital at Luang Prabang (though the administrative capital remained, as in the French period, at Vientiane), Laos entered the period of Asian independence in 1954. It was economically extremely weak, and lacked an adequate elite upon which to base an effective administration. The union under the Luang Prabang dynasty had little appeal to the hill peoples who occupied so much of the country's area. From the outset, Laos was under pressure from the Thais (and their American friends) on the west and the North Vietnamese (presumably with some Chinese support) on the east. It is not surprising that Laos has had a most unhappy history of political instability since the departure of the French.

The modern history of Laos has resulted in the evolution of a new frontier on the South-east Asian mainland. Laotian factions of the right and the centre, with Thai sympathies or American support, have managed to maintain control over most of the wet-rice growing country on the east bank of the Mekong, where lives the bulk of the Lao population. The left factions, led by the Pathet Lao (communists) and enjoying North Vietnamese support, have established a commanding position in the highlands with North Vietnam at their back. The outcome has been the emergence of a kind of double buffer between Thailand and North Vietnam which has no real *de jure* basis—it rests on uneasy political compromises—and which is without doubt extremely unstable. From the American point of view, it is unsatisfactory because it fails to meet one of the major strategic requirements of the Vietnamese crisis: the physical isolation of South Vietnam from North Vietnam. Today, Laotian territory under the control of the Pathet Lao provides a back door into South Vietnam through which, by way of the so-called Ho Chi Minh Trail and other routes, the Viet Cong can receive supplies. Bombing has not closed this door. Military operations on the ground promise greater success, but only at the price of upsetting, perhaps beyond hope of subsequent restabilisation, the Laotian buffer system. The Pathet Lao—and, indeed, all Laotian nationalists, be they of the right or of the left—find the effective partition of Laos extremely distasteful because it involves the undoing of one of the major achievements of French colonial rule: the creation of Laos as a single administrative unit. Laos may not have been such before 1893, but under the French it was. Laotian patriots cannot but look today on their country within the territorial framework of colonial precedent.

CAMBODIA

Unlike Laos, Cambodia managed to enter the colonial era of Asian history with the core of its national identity intact. The present rulers of Cambodia are the heirs of the empire of the Khmers which, until the rise of Thai power in the thirteenth century, was the dominant state of the South-east Asian mainland. In the fifteenth century, the Khmers were obliged under Thai pressure to move their capital south-eastwards from Angkor to the region of Phnom Penh on the lower Mekong, which is still the centre of the Cambodian state. In the sixteenth century, following the southwards march of the Viets from Tonkin into territory which had hitherto been the seat of the Indianised kingdom of the Chams, Cambodia had to face a new threat. During the seventeenth and eighteenth centuries, Cambodia was the prize in a prolonged though episodic struggle between the Thais and the Viets. By the end of the eighteenth century, the Thais had emerged as the dominant power in Cambodia, but in the early nineteenth century the Vietnamese staged a counter-attack. In 1845, a compromise (albeit rather unstable) was reached between the Thais and the Viets. Thailand was confirmed in possession of the western Cambodian provinces in which was situated Angkor and the ancient heart of the Khmer empire. Vietnam acquired the Mekong delta. The remnants of the Cambodian state, centred on Phnom Penh, survived in a tributary relationship with both Hue and Bangkok. Had the prevailing pattern of Cambodian history been allowed to continue without European intervention, even this small vestige of the past greatness of the Khmers would most probably have disappeared and a direct boundary between Thailand and Vietnam would have evolved along a line not far to the west of the Mekong.

There can be no doubt that the French saved Cambodia. In 1863, maintaining that they had assumed traditional Vietnamese rights, the French persuaded King Norodom of Cambodia to place himself under their protection. This guaranteed the survival of the dynasty, though it did not restore to Phnom Penh any influence in the Mekong delta, which the French retained within their colony of Cochin China. The Thais endeavoured to contest the establishment of the French protectorate. Unwilling to face the consequences of a war with the French, however, they accepted in 1867 a compromise in which Thai recognition of the protectorate was exchanged for French confirmation of Thai possession over the former western Cambodian provinces of Siem Reap and Battembang. In the period between 1904 and 1907, the Thais were obliged to retreat a step further, the French taking from them Siem Reap, Battembang and a strip leading to the Gulf of Siam to the east of the Thai port of Chantaburi. These transactions are still much resented in Bangkok, and in 1941 they were reversed for a brief period as one of the Thai spoils of victory in the Franco-Thai war. (See chapter 9.)

With the passing of French rule in 1954, Cambodian leaders believed that they might once more have to face Thai and Vietnamese pressure along their frontiers. Some Vietnamese nationalists have not refrained from questioning the validity of

Cambodian independence. The Thais have, so it seems in Phnom Penh, retained a keen acquisitive interest in Siem Reap and Battembang. These fears go far to explain the present Cambodian neutralism, which is much reinforced by the fact that the Khmers feel no cultural affinity either with the Thais (even though they do share the same brand of Buddhism) or with the Vietnamese (whose Buddhism is of a basically different pattern). Cambodian suspicion of American policy is in no way diminished by the existence of close relations between the United States and the authorities in both Bangkok and Saigon. From the viewpoint of Phnom Penh, it is not too difficult to see how a collapse in the present *status quo* on the South-east Asian mainland might well result in a fresh partition of Cambodia between its eastern and western neighbours.

VIETNAM

Vietnam, which the French came to treat as a single entity, has since 1954 been partitioned between the governments in Saigon and Hanoi. It has become fashionable among the opponents of American policy in South-east Asia to look on this partition as artificial, unnatural and temporary, and they describe the war between the two Vietnamese regimes as a civil war. A study of Vietnamese history, however, shows clearly enough that a divided Vietnam is at least as traditional as a united Vietnam.

The Vietnamese state originated in the Red river delta in Tonkin. In the fifteenth century, under the Le dynasty, the Viets of Tonkin undertook the conquest of Champa: the Indianised kingdom of the Chams, who spoke a Malayo-Polynesian language and whose territory at the height of their power corresponded approximately to the limits of modern South Vietnam. Once they had spread southward, the Viets divided into two distinct and mutually hostile regimes. Under the nominal overlordship of the Le dynasty, Vietnam by the seventeenth century was, in effect, governed by the Trinh dynasty in Tonkin and the Nguyen dynasty in Annam and the south. Between

1620 and 1673, the two dynasties were constantly at war with each other. Then came a century of peace, during which the two Vietnamese states were separated by a wall system (modelled on the Great Wall of China) not far north of the present boundary along the 17th Parallel.

In 1773, the so-called Tay-son rebellion broke out: a Vietnamese civil war in which social discontent played an important role. The Tay-son movement resulted in the destruction of the Trinh in the north and the eclipse of the Nguyen in the south. Once victorious, however, the Tay-son split up into regional fragments. Thus, the Nguyen dynasty—with some outside aid through the French missionary bishop of Adran, Pigneau de Behaine—managed in the last two decades of the eighteenth century not only to overcome the Tay-son power in the south but to defeat it in Tonkin as well. In 1802, the Nguyen ruler, Nguyen Anh, proclaimed himself emperor of a united Vietnam. His title was confirmed by the Chinese emperor, and he then adopted the regnal name Gia Long.

Gia Long's state was the first stable united Vietnamese regime for more than two hundred years, and, because of Vietnamese conquests in the south at the expense of the Chams and the Cambodians, it was a more extensive state than any hitherto known in Vietnamese history. It was this united Vietnam that the French took over between 1858 and 1885. Among the Vietnamese ruling classes, there was a uniformity of culture and administration, based on the Chinese Confucian model, which served to conceal many important differences between the north and the south. From the third century BC, Tonkin had been within the Chinese sphere. At times, as during the T'ang dynasty, it had been under direct Chinese rule. In AD 939 the Vietnamese threw off the Chinese yoke; from that time onwards, except for a few brief periods, they maintained their autonomy right up to the French occupation. Until the European colonial era, however, Vietnamese rulers had been accustomed to seek Chinese confirmation for their title. Both the Trinh and

N

the Nguyen dynasties were Chinese tributaries; up to 1885, the
Chinese exercised a significant measure of influence over the
internal affairs of Tonkin. Chinese influence tended, as one
would expect, to be less important in the south, which was not
in direct territorial contact with metropolitan China. Ethnically
and culturally, moreover, the south was far less Sinicised than
the north. In the Mekong delta, the process of Vietnamisation
of the rural population was still going on in the nineteenth
century, and to this day there are significant cultural differences
between the Red river and Mekong deltas. Under Nguyen rule,
however, these differences tended to be obscured by the Chinese
pattern of government: a process which the French administration did nothing to reverse. For example, one consequence of
the creation of French Indochina was the rise to positions of
power and wealth in the south of Vietnamese families of Ton-
kinese origin, and there remains to this day an extremely
influential northern group in the administration of South Vietnam.

The Viets—that is to say, the speakers of the Vietnamese
language (generally classified as a member of the Austro-
Asiatic group in which also is placed Mon-Khmer)—make up the
overwhelming majority of the population of Vietnam both
North and South. A great deal of the area of Vietnam, however,
is not occupied by Vietnamese speakers. The hill tracts of South
Vietnam are dominated by tribal groups speaking Mon-Khmer
and Cham (Malayo-Polynesian) languages. Outside the Red
river delta in North Vietnam, there exists a crescent of Thai
country stretching from Laos across Vietnam deep into Kwangsi
province in China. Within the Thai areas, there are pockets of
Meo and Yao tribal occupation of hill country.

The pattern of Viet population and Vietnamese civilisation
has to a great extent been determined by factors of economic
geography. The Viets dominate the rice-growing plains and
deltas. They have never settled in hill tracts. Hence, except
in the extreme south in the Mekong delta of South Vietnam and

in the north in the Red river delta of North Vietnam, the Viets have tended, in effect, to confine themselves to a narrow coastal strip in places but a few miles wide. The rice-growing plains of the Viets have lent themselves to the Chinese pattern of government, and the mechanism by which such government has spread down the Indochinese peninsula certainly resembles closely that of the expansion of Chinese civilisation into southern China at an earlier period. The Chinese administrative forms which took root in the Viet-occupied plains did not spread so easily into the hills. Today, both Vietnams—and particularly South Vietnam—are divided into two distinct cultural zones: the Viet lowlands and the non-Viet hill tracts. In the case of both North and South Vietnam, the non-Viet hill country overflows westwards into Laos. For much of its length, the present boundary between Laos and Vietnam represents no real cultural or ethnic divide, but follows a convenient watershed line separating streams flowing into the Mekong on the one hand and the South China Sea on the other. There would seem to be more problems involved in the unification of Vietnam than the reconciliation of the Northern Viets with the Southern Viets. One solution, to which there can be no doubt that much thought has been given in both Hanoi and Saigon, lies in a Viet political domination of eastern Laos and Cambodia, bringing the bulk of the tribal hills into the Vietnamese sphere.

Under French administration, Vietnam—though for practical purposes generally treated as a unity—was, in fact, divided into three parts: the colony of Cochin China and the protectorates of Annam and Tonkin. The centres of French power were Saigon in the south and Hanoi in the north. At Hue, the old capital of the empire of Annam, the descendants of the Nguyen dynasty were allowed to linger on in obscurity. In March 1945, the Nguyen dynasty was given a final, and brief, opportunity to unite Vietnam when the Japanese overthrew the Vichy French regime in Indochina and persuaded the royal heir, Bao Dai, to declare Vietnam independent under his leadership. The outcome, instead of unity, was to be a series of partitions culminating in the 1954 Geneva settlement. The first stage was the refusal of Ho Chi Minh—who, at the war's end, was in effective control of most of Tonkin—to accept on behalf of his party, the Vietminh, any regime headed by Bao Dai. The next stage was set by the actual process of the Japanese surrender. According to decisions made at the Potsdam Conference, it was agreed that in Indochina (Laos as well as Vietnam) the Chinese forces of Chiang Kai-shek should take the Japanese surrender down to the 16th Parallel, below which point responsibility would be in British hands. In the Chinese zone the Vietminh were supported; in the British zone they were not.

When the French eventually returned to Vietnam in force in early 1946, they were able to regain control of the south but experienced extreme difficulty in dislodging Ho Chi Minh and the Vietminh from the north. At first the French were inclined to accept a partition under their general supervision, but by the end of 1946 they had come into armed conflict with the Vietminh—one bone of contention being the political future of the French colony of Cochin China, which it was the policy of Paris to keep separate from the protectorates of Annam and Tonkin. In 1949, the French at last agreed to merge Cochin China (that is to say, the Saigon region and the Mekong delta) into a united Vietnam headed by the Emperor Bao Dai. This measure, however, failed to satisfy the Vietminh and to undo the partition of 1945. In 1954, after the defeat at Dienbienphu, the French were obliged to accept the inevitable. Vietnam was divided into two regimes. Ho Chi Minh and the Vietminh controlled the northern part of the former protectorate. The southern part at first remained under Bao Dai, in theory still the ruler of all Vietnam; but in 1955, Bao Dai was formally deposed and the southern part became the Republic of South Vietnam. The Geneva agreements of 1954 made reference to the holding of pan-Vietnamese elections which might lead to the reunification of the country. No intelligent observer, however, could have escaped the conclusion that the end of French rule had, in fact, once more divided Vietnam in the traditional pattern established during the period of Trinh-Nguyen dynastic conflict. This partition, of course, was now complicated by a factor quite absent in the seventeenth and eighteenth centuries; the divide was now ideological as well as geographical. The regime in the North was communist, while the ruling groups who dominated the South were strongly anti-communist.

From a geopolitical point of view, there is a great deal to be said in favour of the 1954 partition. The Viets are very much the odd-men-out in mainland South-east Asia, Sinicised rather than Indianised. Tonkin is without question a Chinese frontier zone, and China will always try to maintain its influence there and exclude that of other powers. To add the South to Tonkin is to extend the potential area of Chinese influence around the eastern flank of the Indianised South-east Asian mainland. Were Vietnam possessed of a dominant Indianised civilisation, like Burma, the consequences might be of lesser import. The Chinese are unlikely to absorb the Burmese people even though they may dominate Burmese foreign policy. The Chinese, however, could well absorb the Viets of Vietnam, the southernmost of the Yüeh peoples, just as they have absorbed the other Yüeh states in south China. Vietnam is the one direction in South-east Asia in which it would be easy to see a future advance of the Chinese boundary. This is not to say that such an advance is, unless opposed, inevitable; simply that it is theoretically possible, according to the established pattern of Chinese frontier evolution in this quarter over the millennia. There is no evidence to suggest that the North Vietnamese actually *want* to come under Chinese control, and a great deal of evidence to indicate that they do not.

On this analysis, Vietnam can be seen as analogous to those territories which lay between two advancing European empires in the nineteenth century—like Iran, for example, confronted by the approach of Russia from the Caucasus and Transcaspia, and of the British from Baluchistan. In the case of Iran, the consequences of direct imperial contact were avoided by the conversion of the country into a buffer, with clearly defined spheres of influence. Vietnam, too, could serve as a buffer between China and the anti-communist influences in South-east Asia. Tonkin—North Vietnam—would be the Chinese side of the buffer, and South Vietnam the Western or anti-communist side. In so far as it aims to create such a buffer, American policy in Vietnam has much logic behind it. If China's side of the buffer, North Vietnam, turned out to be resistant to direct Chinese influence—in other words, Titoist in outlook—then this would only serve to increase the utility of the buffer system as a whole.

It is at this point that we can see the main impact of the colonial legacy. All arguments about the traditional division of Vietnam into two regions cannot eliminate the fact that, under French rule, Vietnam was, in practice if not in theory, united. The leaders of both South and North, having lived through the period of the struggle against the French, see themselves as the heirs to the united Vietnamese state created by the French. They feel about a divided Vietnam much as many Indian leaders, albeitly tacitly, feel about the partition of the Indian subcontinent. A united Vietnam may not be desirable on strategic grounds; the traditional basis for it may not have been as well-established as might at first sight be supposed; yet the imperial precedent has been created and cannot be forgotten.

★

It may well be that the final settlement of the Vietnam problem will bring with it a permanent partition. If so, then this will mean a major change in the boundary system of French Indochina, and it could lead to other changes in that system in Laos and Cambodia. Some theoretical possibilities have already been indicated here. In the last analysis, it can be said that the French boundary system was designed with the British empire

in mind. The present limits of Laos and Cambodia were closely
related to the expansion of British Burma. Thailand remained
independent because it was a convenient Anglo-French buffer.
Today, however, the problem is no longer how to keep the
British and French apart, but how to keep the Chinese and the
West from establishing a common boundary with all the con-
sequent tensions. In other words, the buffer system has in
recent years been turned through an angle of 90 degrees. Can it,
in this new position, function satisfactorily with its boundaries
unmodified and its pattern of sovereignties unchanged?

I I

Russia, China and Mongolia

Unlike Britain and France, Russia has managed to retain its empire in Asia. There was a period of crisis following the outbreak of the Bolshevik Revolution in 1917, when it looked as if many of the Russian Asiatic possessions would pass out of the control of Moscow; but by the end of the 1920s, the Soviet central government had re-established its authority. There was no independence in Russian Turkestan; Russian frontier guards still stood along the north bank of the Amur. There were to be periods when it seemed as if Soviet Russia had not only retained the tsarist territories in the east but had also inherited tsarist ambitions for expansion in Sinkiang, Inner Mongolia and Manchuria. Hence, along the land boundaries of Russia beyond the Urals, there has been a far more obvious continuity of frontier policy in modern times than has been the case along the boundaries of the successor states to British India and French Indochina.

The Chinese empire, also, has fared well in the age of Asian decolonisation, and particularly so following the victory of the Chinese communists in 1949. Chinese power in Tibet and Sinkiang is probably greater today than it has ever been before.

Regions which were traditionally regarded as protectorates, free from direct Chinese administration, have now been incorporated into the governmental structure of China proper. The trend, of course, was set during the latter years of Manchu rule, but it is the Chinese communists who have developed it to its present stage. Of all the major Chinese-influenced frontier tracts beyond the Wall, only Outer Mongolia has evolved away from China's sphere into a state of full independence. Outer Mongolia, now, is the only buffer between areas under direct Chinese and Russian rule. Along the rest of the long Sino-Russian border, from the Pamirs to the Pacific Ocean, Russians and Chinese face each other. (See Map 27.)

Theorists of imperial frontier policy would have found exceedingly unsatisfactory the present situation on the Sino-Russian border. Direct contact between two great powers would surely lead to much friction and tension. To some extent, this has proved to be the case in practice. The territorial juxtaposition of the two great communist powers in Asia has done nothing to ease the troubled course of their mutual relations, and it has served to complicate and embitter differences of an ideological nature.

The Sino-Russian boundary can be divided into three sectors. First: there is the boundary between the Russian Tadzhik, Kirgiz and Kazakh republics on the one hand, and Chinese Sinkiang on the other. Second: there is the buffer zone of Mongolia (Outer Mongolia) with its Russian and Chinese boundaries. Third: there is the boundary between Russia and Manchuria. Along each of these sectors, the Russians extended their influence during the tsarist era. (See Maps 28, 29 and 30.)

THE SINKIANG SECTOR

The Russian boundary with Sinkiang (or Chinese Turkestan as the region was generally called before the 1880s) evolved in the second half of the nineteenth century mainly as a result of the creation of Russian Turkestan. The Sino-Russian Protocol

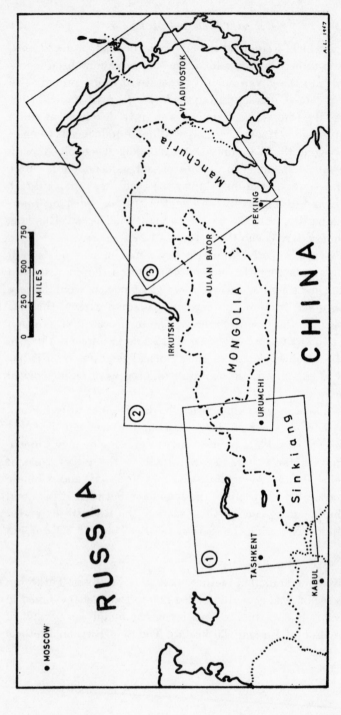

27. The Sino-Russian border: 1. Sinkiang sector; 2. Mongolian sector; 3. Manchurian sector.

of Chuguchak (or Tarbagatai) in 1864 defined the eastern end of
this boundary: the section between the Dzungarian region of
Sinkiang and what is now the Kazakh republic. The basis
accepted (and already laid down in principle in the Peking
Treaty of 1860) was that the line of Chinese pickets—posts set
up to control nomad movement—should represent the boundary. There existed considerable uncertainty as to the location
of the pickets, some of which were far from permanent and were
shifted over considerable distances according to local needs and
Chinese strength and energy. Arguing on the basis of the line
of the most remote of the temporary and moveable pickets, the
Chinese in 1864 could probably have produced a territorial
definition which gave them the entire basin of the Zaysan Lake
and at least the eastern shores of Lake Balkash. The Russians,
however, were able to interpret the 1864 boundary as following
a line farther to the south and west: a line marked by permanent
Chinese posts and situated well back from the farthest limits of
Chinese influence. This boundary was reinforced in the Sino-
Russian Treaty of St Petersburg of 1881. The difference between
the boundary which the Russians secured and that which the
Chinese might have claimed on the basis of the outermost line
of temporary pickets, is said to represent as much as 350,000
square miles of territory.*

The Treaty of St Petersburg was a product of the period from
1864 to the late 1870s, when Chinese Turkestan, under the
leadership of the Kokandi adventurer, Yakub Beg, threw off
the Manchu yoke. In 1871, the Russians—on the grounds that
they needed to protect themselves against the disturbed state
of transfrontier tracts—took advantage of the Chinese collapse

---

* That is, if one ignores some of the more extreme claims shown on
Chinese maps of both Kuomintang and communist times. One such
map, in *Chung-kuo sang-ti shih* (A History of China's Lost Territory) by
Hsieh Pin, Shanghai 1925, shows the entire Kazakh nomad territory,
stretching to the west of the Aral Sea, as being Chinese by rights. (See
Map 6, page 30)

to occupy the lower Ili valley in Dzungaria, including the Chinese administrative centre of Kuldja. In 1881, following a crisis which threatened to produce a Sino-Russian war with wider international implications, the Russians gave up Kuldja and most of the Ili valley, though they managed to retain a few small tracts which had been Chinese on the eve of the Yakub Beg crisis. The transaction was embodied in the Treaty of St Petersburg, which also dealt with a wide range of topics relating to the Sino-Russian border and trade across it. Chinese public opinion at the time was much incensed by the 1881 agreement, which Chinese writers have ever since included in their lists of 'unequal' treaties imposed upon them by the imperial powers.

In 1882–85, as an outcome of the 1881 treaty, the boundary between Sinkiang ('New Dominion' as Chinese Turkestan was renamed in 1883) and what are now the Kirgiz and Kazakh republics of the USSR was demarcated on the ground. In the west, demarcation stopped at the Uzbel pass on the northern fringe of the Pamirs. In 1895, following the Anglo-Russian agreement over the Russo-Afghan boundary in the Pamirs, the Sino-Russian boundary from the Uzbel pass southwards to Afghan Wakhan was settled *de facto* along the line of the Aksu-Sarikol watershed. China, which possessed claims to tracts in the Pamirs to the west of this line, based mainly on Chinese military operations in the middle of the eighteenth century, did not participate in the Pamirs settlement. Chinese writers of all political persuasions still maintain that, in 1895, China was deprived of many thousands of square miles of territory in the Pamirs. In 1901, it looked as if the Russians intended to cross the Aksu-Sarikol watershed when they established a military post at Tashkurgan, just to its east. Despite the crisis of the Chinese Revolution in Sinkiang in 1912, when the Russians despatched considerable forces to their consulates at Kashgar and elsewhere, the Aksu-Sarikol watershed line remained the effective frontier. By 1917, the Tashgurgan post had been withdrawn. The boundary from the Uzbel pass to

28. The Sinkiang sector of the Sino-Russian border.

Wakhan, however, has yet to be demarcated by joint Russo-Chinese action.*

Since 1895, there has been little doubt as to the effective line of the border between Russia and Sinkiang, and the Russians appear to have made no serious efforts to modify that line.

* The demarcation of the Sino-Afghan border in 1964 may, perhaps, be construed to imply a Chinese acceptance of the Aksu-Sarikol divide as its border with Russia in the Pamirs. The text of the Sino-Afghan boundary agreement of 1963 does not appear to have been published, so it is impossible to comment on the terms with which the northern terminus of that boundary was described. This point, however, must coincide closely with the old Russian-Afghan border terminus of 1895.

There have been periods since 1895, however, when the status of Sinkiang itself has been in question. In 1912, as has already been noted, the Russians reinforced their consular guards in the region—a protective measure, they said, called for by the uncertainties and turbulence of the Chinese Revolution—and there were many foreign observers (including the British representative in Kashgar, Sir George Macartney) who saw this as the prelude to a Russian annexation of all Sinkiang. In the late 1930s, during the government of Sinkiang by Sheng Shih-ts'ai —at that time much under Soviet influence—it again seemed as if the region was about to come under Russian 'protection'. By 1940, Russia had acquired a virtual monopoly of the exploitation of minerals in Sinkiang including petroleum. In 1942, however, Sheng Shih-ts'ai broke with Moscow and went over to the Kuomintang. The Russians at first seemed willing to accept this reverse, and by 1944 they had withdrawn their technicians and equipment from the Sinkiang oilfields. By the end of that year, however, there was evidence to suggest that they had not, in fact, abandoned all their interests in Sinkiang and that they were assisting a separatist regime—the so-called Republic of Eastern Turkestan, based on Kuldja (Ining)—in that Ili region which had been under Russian occupation from 1871 to 1881. The Kuldja regime disappeared with the advent to power of the Chinese communists in 1949, and with it went the last Soviet political foothold in Sinkiang.

In Soviet times, as in the tsarist era, Russian influence in and concern with Sinkiang tended to increase in periods when the control of the region by the Chinese central government was weak. Soviet support for Sheng Shih-ts'ai was really an extension of the kind of tsarist frontier policy which had brought Russian rule into the territory of the Central Asian khanates in the 1860s and 1870s. The Kuomintang, like the Manchus before it, was never quite strong enough in Sinkiang to allay Russian anxieties as to the consequences of transfrontier disturbances. It was just strong enough, however, to prevent such anxieties giving rise to permanent military occupation. Thus, an uneasy balance was retained. The Chinese communists, from the outset, possessed far more power in the region than had either the Manchus or the Kuomintang. However, they still had to face a major problem of administration which had confronted their predecessors: the question of the Sinkiang indigenous population, containing Islamic Turkic groups like the Uighurs and the Kazakhs. It was anti-Chinese rebellion by such people which, in the nineteenth century, created the disturbed conditions in Chinese Turkestan providing the occasion for the Russian occupation of the Ili in 1871–81; and it was discontent among the non-Chinese in Sinkiang in the 1930s and 1940s which provided the background for Soviet influence in the region. Should the present Chinese regime ever lose control of its Sinkiang minorities, then Russia could hardly avoid once more taking an active interest in events beyond this border. With a Kazakh population of over 3 million, Russia could hardly ignore an anti-Chinese rebellion by the 500,000 or so Kazakhs in Sinkiang. It is perhaps significant, in this context, that the Sino-Russian border on the Ili, which divides Russian and Chinese Kazakhs, has, since the opening of the 1960s, been the scene of a large number of 'incidents'. Since 1964, the Chinese have issued repeated warnings to Russia not to meddle in Kazakh affairs in Sinkiang, and, in particular, not to encourage Kazakhs in China to migrate across the border to join their Soviet brethren.

Hitherto, Sinkiang has been a sparsely populated tract on the Russian frontier. Modern Chinese policy may well convert it into a region of active Chinese ethnic settlement adjacent to relatively unpopulated Russian territory. Whereas, in the past, it has been the Russians who have been pressing eastwards and southwards along the borders of Sinkiang, with increasing Chinese population the direction of pressure might well change. Demographic considerations might perhaps lead the Chinese to more than theoretical thoughts on the modification of the

Sino-Russian border as it was established during the course of the nineteenth century. Some observers have, in this context, pointed to the recent Chinese emphasis (e.g., *People's Daily* of March 8, 1963) that the 1881 Treaty of St Petersburg, with its definition of the Sino-Russian border on the Ili, is as 'unequal' as any of the other 'unequal' treaties included in catalogues of imperialist aggression at the expense of the Chinese people.

China has three theoretical objections to the Russo-Sinkiang boundary in its present form. First: by virtue of their contacts with the Kazakhs and other nomad groups in Manchu times, the Chinese could claim that they had acquired rights over tribal territory in the neighbourhood of the Balkhash, Uch-Aral and Zaysan lakes—all now within the Soviet Union. Second: the Chinese have never been happy with the Ili boundary defined in the treaty of 1881. The Russians, by this agreement, retained some territory which they had acquired as a result of their occupation of the Ili in 1871; and the Chinese have consistently felt that the boundary here should revert to its pre-1871 alignment. Third: in the Pamirs, the Russians in the early 1890s occupied the grazing lands of nomads who also possessed some kind of tributary relationship to the Chinese authorities at Kashgar. In the mid-eighteenth century, Manchu forces had penetrated a considerable distance to the west of the Aksu-Sarikol watershed line, which became the *de facto* Sino-Russian boundary in 1895.

If taken to extremes, the potential area of China's claim could amount to several hundred thousand square miles. In practice, however, the Chinese have for more than half a century offered no serious challenge to Russian rule in the Pamirs; and along the Ili and the Kazakh republic's border, despite much Peking talk, crises have, in effect, been largely confined to those arising from problems of frontier administration and control.

THE OUTER MONGOLIAN SECTOR

To the east of Sinkiang lies Outer Mongolia. In the eighteenth and nineteenth centuries, the Manchu dynasty maintained its influence here by a system of protection and indirect rule. In the early twentieth century, however, the Manchu policy underwent a change, in part as a response to imperial pressures on the Chinese frontiers. An attempt was made to push Chinese colonists beyond Inner Mongolia into Outer Mongolia and, ultimately, to bring all Mongolia under direct Chinese administration. The Mongols much resented this development. In 1911, with the outbreak of the Chinese Revolution, Outer Mongolia lost no time in declaring itself independent of Chinese rule.

By the first half of the seventeenth century, the Russians had come into direct contact with territory inhabited by Mongol tribes. Some tribes, members of the western Mongol group, migrated to Russian Siberia, where they settled under tsarist protection. Another Mongol group, the Buriats of the Lake Baikal region, endeavoured to oppose the Russian advance and were conquered. By the end of the seventeenth century, there were Russian outposts along the greater part of what is today the border between the Soviet Union and the Mongolian People's Republic; and this line, from the Sayan mountains to the Argun river (a tributary of the Amur), was recognised as the Sino-Russian boundary in the Treaty of Kiakhta of 1727: an agreement which also permitted Russian trade across the border into Chinese territory. During the second half of the nineteenth century, Russian influence in Outer Mongolia increased with the decline in power of the Manchus; and it was this influence that the new Chinese policy of Mongolian colonisation was designed to counter.

With the development of the Russian Far East, and particularly after construction of the Trans-Siberian Railway was started in the last decade of the nineteenth century, the Russo-Mongolian border acquired a special strategic significance. Chinese power, if firmly established along its southern side, would threaten the main Russian line of communication which, in the region of Lake Baikal, ran less than a hundred miles north

o

of the frontier. And there existed the more than theoretical
possibility that, one day, the place of the Chinese might be
taken by the Japanese. Thus the Russians had good reasons for
their opposition to late Manchu policy in Mongolia: reasons
which have remained valid to the present day. The outbreak of

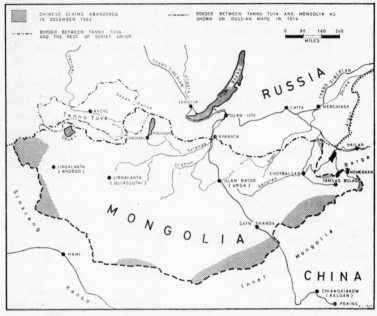

29. The Mongolian sector of the Sino-Russian border.

the Chinese Revolution in 1911 gave the Russians an opportunity to secure their Mongolian flank. It also presented them
with a major policy dilemma. The Mongolian revolutionary
leaders sought complete independence from China and they
wanted, moreover, all Mongol areas—even those outside the
traditional limits of Outer Mongolia—to be included within the
new Mongol state. They argued that Inner Mongolia and Barga
(administratively in Manchuria) should join the regime they
were trying to set up in Urga. Russia, while supporting the

Mongolian revolutionaries, yet felt that a total removal of Outer Mongolia from the Chinese sphere would arouse opposition from the major powers and would probably lead to war with China. Similar consequences would probably flow from any attempt to add Inner Mongolia and Barga to Outer Mongolia, even if the combined region was accepted as being under Chinese suzerainty of some kind. Thus, the Mongolian revolutionaries had to be restrained from attempting to create a pan-Mongol state, and were obliged to accept a lesser status than that which they had originally sought. Outer Mongolia was to be autonomous, but to remain in some way part of Chinese territory: a status which may be compared to that which the British endeavoured to create for Outer Tibet during the Simla Conference of 1913–14. An autonomous Outer Mongolia on this pattern was recognised by Russo-Chinese declaration in 1913 and by tripartite Russo-Mongol-Chinese agreement in 1915. During this period, moreover, the Russians detached from Outer Mongolia the district of Urianghai, or Tannu Tuva, which they then placed under their own protection. This step—which might perhaps be construed as a major modification of the Russian border as it was implied in the Treaty of Chuguchak of 1864—had a certain logic behind it, since the Urianghai are a Turkic people, distinct from the Mongols, and have implicitly been recognised as such in Sino-Russian treaties dating back to 1727.

With the fall of the tsarist regime in Russia, the Chinese attempted to re-establish their influence in Outer Mongolia. In 1919, they sent troops into the region and, by the decree of the president of the Chinese republic, they cancelled Mongolian autonomy. However, in 1921, with some White Russian support, the Mongols expelled the Chinese and in the following year Soviet forces destroyed the White Russian faction. In 1924, Outer Mongolia declared itself fully independent as the Mongolian People's Republic, and was recognised as such by the Soviet Union. Meanwhile, the Soviets had turned Urianghai into the 'Republic of Tannu Tuva', nominally independent but in effect a Russian satellite. Mongolia accepted this *fait accompli* in 1926, when a treaty of friendship was signed by the People's Republic of Tannu Tuva and the Mongolian People's Republic. As a reward for their agreement to the loss of Tannu Tuva— some 80,000 square miles in area—the Mongols were given Darkhat: a small strip along the new border west of Lake Khobso Gol. In 1944, Tannu Tuva was formally incorporated within the Soviet Union. The Chinese republic was never reconciled to the permanent loss of Outer Mongolia and Urianghai (Tannu Tuva). While Chiang Kai-shek, under Russian pressure, acknowledged Mongolian independence in 1946, there continued to be published official Chinese maps which showed both Outer Mongolia and Urianghai as forming part of the dominions of the Chinese republic. In 1950, the new communist regime in Peking signed an agreement with the Soviet Union in which the full independence of the Mongolian People's Republic was recognised.

The boundary between Russia and Outer Mongolia was defined clearly enough during the course of the eighteenth, nineteenth and early twentieth centuries. In 1924, however, at the time of the formal creation of the Mongolian People's Republic, there existed rather less certainty as to the alignment of the boundary between Outer Mongolia and Chinese territory. There were extensive disputed tracts along the border between Outer Mongolia and Chinese territory in Sinkiang, Inner Mongolia and Manchuria. Provision for Sino-Mongol boundary demarcation by joint commission had been made in the Russo-Chinese declaration of 1913 and the Russo-Mongol-Chinese agreement of 1915, but no verbal definition had been attempted. Under the Chinese republic, no Sino-Mongol boundary commission completed its task. In 1962, however, the Chinese communists settled with the Mongolian People's Republic the alignment of all their common border, in the majority of instances abandoning Chinese claims in favour of the Mongols. No doubt this act of delimitation was expedited by the prevailing atmosphere of Sino-Russian rivalry; and the fact that much of the terrain involved formed part of the Gobi desert probably helped as well. By agreeing to a defined Sino-Mongol border, it may be presumed that the Mongolian People's Republic has abandoned its territorial hopes in Inner Mongolia where, by 1962, the Mongols had become heavily outnumbered by Han Chinese settlers.

From the opening of the nineteenth century, Mongolia became part of the zone of Russo-Japanese competition and, in effect, it served as a buffer for Russia against Japan as well as China : part of the screen between Russian Siberia and Far East and the Japanese spheres of interest in Inner Mongolia and Manchuria. Secret Russo-Japanese agreements of 1907 and 1912 confirmed Russian rights and interests in Outer Mongolia while defining the position of both powers in Inner Mongolia. In the late 1930s, however, the Japanese, having entrenched themselves firmly in both Manchuria and Inner Mongolia, began to press hard on the frontiers of the Russian sphere. One consequence was the outbreak of armed clashes between the Soviets and the Japanese Kwangtung army along the Amur in 1938. Another consequence was a Japanese probe intended, it would seem, to pinch out that salient of Outer Mongolia between Barga and Inner Mongolia. The Soviet government rallied to the defence of the frontiers of the Mongolian People's Republic. Heavy fighting took place during the summer of 1939, and the Japanese were rebuffed. The outcome was the Japanese recognition, in 1942, of the old Mongolian boundary, the defences of which the Russians hastened to strengthen by the construction of a strategic railway from Chita on the Trans-Siberian line to Tamtsak Bulak, near the extreme eastern tip of the Mongolian People's Republic. Tamtsak Bulak provided the launching point for the Russian invasion of Manchuria in 1945 on the eve of the Japanese surrender, and it remains today the obvious base for any Russian project for a drive to the Gulf of Chihli to cut China off from the heartland of its industrialisation.

Mongolia, though influenced and controlled to a varying

degree by Soviet policy since 1924, is certainly today something more than a Russian puppet-state. As Sino-Soviet competition continues, so no doubt will the Mongolian People's Republic increasingly have the opportunity to balance one neighbour against another, much as Nepal balances Indian and Chinese influences, and as Afghanistan used to balance the influences of the British and the Russians. The Chinese would no doubt like to increase their influence in the Mongolian People's Republic, if only to eliminate the strategic threat posed by the Tamtsak Bulak railway to which reference has already been made; and there can be no question that the Chinese communists, like their Kuomintang predecessors, hope that one day Outer Mongolia will rejoin the Chinese fold. The Mongols of Inner Mongolia are one of the major ethnic minority groups in the Chinese People's Republic, symbolised by one of the five stars on the present Chinese flag. But, however much China's present leaders might long for the union of the Outer Mongols with the Inner Mongols, there is very little evidence to suggest that they plan at this time to consummate it by force. It seems likely that, for the time being, both Russian and Chinese strategists appreciate the value of the buffer properties of the Mongolian People's Republic.

THE MANCHURIAN SECTOR

The final stretch of the Sino-Russian boundary runs from Mongolia to the Sea of Japan, just south of the Russian port of Vladivostok. The greater part of this alignment is defined by the course of the Amur river and its tributaries, the Argun and the Ussuri. The Russians first began to explore the Amur basin in the 1640s, and in 1665 they founded the fortified settlement at Albazin on the Amur, opposite what today would be the most northerly point of Manchuria. Albazin became the base for the expansion of Russian settlement down the Amur valley. The Russians came to the Amur at the moment when the Manchus were in the process of taking over China from the Ming dynasty; it was not until 1652 that the Manchus decided to offer armed resistance to Russia's encroachment towards the northern borders of their homeland and its assumption of sovereignty over Tungusic tribes which had hitherto been accepted as Manchu dependants. There followed three decades of occasional Sino-Manchu armed encounters and abortive negotiation. The Russians were from time to time checked only to renew their advance. In 1681, the Emperor K'ang-hsi, having at last put down a series of anti-Manchu rebellions in south China, decided to meet the Russians with major forces and to put an end, once and for all, to their progress down the Amur and their assumption of rule over Tungusic tribes owing allegiance to the Manchus. Serious operations began in 1683. The advanced Russian settlements were destroyed and Albazin was besieged in 1685 and again in 1686. Though the Russians managed to hold Albazin, the determination of the Chinese opposition convinced them of the wisdom of negotiations; these were initiated with the assistance of Jesuit missionaries resident in Peking, and culminated in the Sino-Russian Treaty of Nerchinsk of 1689.

By the Treaty of Nerchinsk, the Russians gave up Albazin and their Amur settlements to its east. A Sino-Russian boundary was defined which ran from the Amur west of Albazin, along the crests of the Yablonovoi and Stanovoi mountains, to the Sea of Okhotsk south of the mouth of the Ud river. The greater part of this line, and particularly its eastern end, passed through country on which neither the Chinese nor the Russians possessed accurate topographical information, and its description in the text of the Treaty of Nerchinsk was, accordingly, rather vague. Further discussions in 1727 failed to produce significant clarification. There could exist no doubt, however, that the 1689 boundary excluded the Russians from all but the extreme north-western corner of the Amur basin, and that it met the Pacific Ocean at a point more than 700 miles to the north of what is today the great port of Vladivostok.

The Nerchinsk line held until the 1850s, when it was breached by the energetic policy of Nikolai Muraviev, the Russian governor-general of Eastern Siberia. Muraviev, who took up his appointment in 1847, by 1860 had added more than 300,000 square miles to the dominions of the tsar. Beginning with

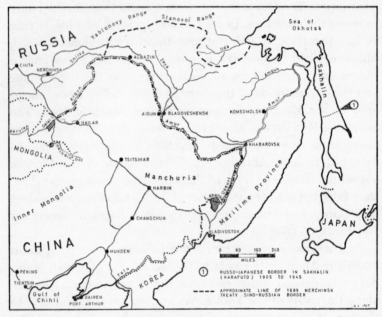

30. The Manchurian sector of the Sino-Russian border.

exploration and the establishment of outposts, by 1854 Muraviev was sending flotillas of barges down the Amur from the Russian frontier, deep into what had hitherto been accepted as Chinese territory. An advanced Russian base was established at Khabarovsk at the junction of the Amur and the Ussuri. In May 1858, taking advantage of the growing crisis in Chinese relations with the British and the French, Muraviev met Chinese representatives at Aigun on the middle reach of the

Amur, and secured recognition of the Russian acquisition of
the north bank of the Amur eastwards to its junction with the
Ussuri. It was further agreed that the territory between the
Ussuri and the Pacific coast should be considered to be owned
jointly by Russia and China until, at some later date, its final
disposition was settled. Lastly, the Aigun agreement permitted
the Chinese government to retain jurisdiction over sixty-four
Manchu settlements on the north bank of the Amur: that is to
say, on the Russian side. Not taking account of the tract
between the Ussuri and the Pacific, the Aigun boundary gave
Russia some 185,000 square miles of territory which had been
recognised as being Chinese in 1689. In 1859, the Chinese
repudiated the Aigun agreement. In the following year, however, the Russian diplomatist, General Nikolai Ignatiev, was
able to assume the posture of mediator between the Chinese and
the Anglo-French forces which had fought their way to Peking.
As his reward, in November 1860, Ignatiev secured the Treaty
of Peking which reaffirmed the Aigun agreement of 1858 and
improved on it by omitting all reference to Chinese control over
the sixty-four settlements on the north bank of the Amur,* and
by gaining for Russia exclusive possession of the land between
the Ussuri and the Pacific: a tract of some 130,000 square miles
which was to become known as the Maritime Province. In fact,
this was already in Russian hands, and, before the Treaty of
Peking was signed, Muraviev had founded there the port of
Vladivostok, the name of which means in Russian 'Rule of the
East'—which indicated well enough the ambitions of the
government of Eastern Siberia.

Muraviev's advance, which was very much the result of his

---

* The Chinese, however, appear to have retained some control over
these settlements until 1900 when, with the outbreak of the Boxer
troubles, the Russians entered Manchuria in force. The inhabitants of
these settlements, which were concentrated in the region of Blagovesh-
chensk, were then expelled by the Russians, some 5,000 Chinese subjects
being slaughtered in the process.

own initiative and only accepted by his superiors in St Petersburg when it was already a *fait accompli*, involved territory which was sparsely inhabited by Tungus forest people. It had been Manchu policy to check the process of Chinese colonisation in Manchuria; by the middle of the nineteenth century, while a few Chinese were to be found in villages along the Amur, by no stretch of the imagination could the new Russian acquisitions be described as regions of Chinese settlement. With the Russian advance, however, Manchu policy was revised. The second half of the nineteenth century saw the beginning of a great expansion in the Chinese population of Manchuria: a process which was to be accelerated by the development of railways. The rise of towns in Russian territory, like Khabarovsk and Vladivostok, also provided a potential magnet for Chinese settlement and a continuing problem in Russian frontier administration. From the outset, it was Russian policy to check Chinese immigration; and Chinese settlers on Russian soil have not had a happy history. In 1939, there were reported to have been nearly 90,000 Chinese living under Soviet rule in Siberia. In post-war census statistics, this population seems to have vanished into thin air.

The Russian gains of 1858–60 produced a frontier with Manchuria which, for all but the last few miles at its eastern extremity, followed the course of the Amur and Ussuri rivers. Apart from minor questions concerning islands and river-bed fluctuations, this alignment has been unambiguous and provides the most logical natural frontier to be found in the region. However, by the end of the nineteenth century, it had become obvious that there were influential Russian political groups which did not see the Amur-Ussuri line as the final limit of Russia's expansion in this quarter. With the decline of the power of the Manchu dynasty—demonstrated beyond doubt by the outcome of the Sino-Japanese war in 1895—the whole of Manchuria and Korea appeared to be within the grasp of a Russia whose power in the Far East, as the Trans-Siberian Railway neared completion, was steadily increasing. In 1898, the Russians secured a twenty-five-year lease (which was really but a veiled annexation) of Port Arthur and some 1,300 square miles of the Liaotung peninsula in southern Manchuria; and, in 1900, with the outbreak of the Boxer rising in China, they occupied the rest of Manchuria. Russian ambitions in Manchuria, however, came into direct conflict with those of Japan. The outcome of the Russo-Japanese war in 1905 marked a decisive check to Russia's expansion in the Far East and a forced retreat to the 1858–60 frontier line. Even so, there is much evidence to suggest that the Russians—tsarist and communist alike—did not abandon all thought of territorial acquisition in Manchuria until after the victory over the Kuomintang of the Chinese communists in 1949. During 1945–46, after Japan's defeat in the Second World War, the Russians again occupied Manchuria, and there were Russian troops stationed in the Port Arthur region until 1954. While the Second World War did not result in any lasting Russian territorial acquisitions in Manchuria, it nevertheless produced some expansion in the Far East; for, in 1945, the Russians took the southern part of Sakhalin island, which had been recognised as Japanese since the Treaty of Portsmouth ending the Russo-Japanese war in 1905.*

★

During the first years of the Soviet regime, there were some bolshevik leaders who doubted the morality of Russia's continuing to enjoy the fruits of tsarist expansion at the expense of the Chinese. In the so-called Karakhan Declaration of 1919 the bolsheviks declared void all tsarist treaties with China and renounced all concessions and territory which had been 'ravenously' taken from China 'by the tsar's government and by the

---

* By the Russo-Japanese agreement signed at Shimoda in 1855, Sakhalin was defined as being under some vague kind of Russo-Japanese condominion. In 1875, the Russians took over the whole island, but in 1905 had to surrender the southern half below the 50th Parallel, which the Japanese knew as Karafuto.

Russian bourgeoisie'.* In 1924 the Soviet government made an agreement with the Kuomintang for the 'redemarcation' of the Sino-Russian border, the implication possibly being that tsarist wrongs would thereby be rectified. The agreement, however, made it clear that, pending such redemarcation, the existing (that is to say, tsarist) boundaries would remain in being. By 1949, there could be no doubt that, regardless of questions of socialist morality, the Russian government had decided that the *de facto* boundary with China was the boundary to which it would adhere. To this boundary, moreover, it would seem that the Chinese communist leadership had reconciled itself in 1949.

Since the development of the great Sino-Soviet argument began in the late 1950s, signs have emerged from China of a challenge to the alignment of the Sino-Soviet border. Chinese maps have been published which imply claims to Soviet territory in Kazakhstan and the Pamirs. The validity of the treaties of Aigun, Peking and St Petersburg—'unequal' treaties of the worst kind—has been contested in the Chinese press. All this has been accompanied by an interminable series of 'incidents', mainly along the Kazakhstan-Sinkiang border and particularly in the Ili region, though no stretch of the long Sino-Soviet boundary has been entirely trouble-free in recent years. There can be no doubt that both the Russians and the Chinese have devoted considerable military resources to the defence of their mutual frontiers: a fact which in no way diminishes the likelihood of incidents.

Is it Chinese policy today to strive for the recovery of the territory lost to Russia during the second half of the nineteenth century? Does Peking really intend one day to push the Russians back from the Amur to the Nerchinsk line of 1689, to take over the great port of Vladivostok and to advance into Kazakhstan and the Pamirs? Or is it that these boundary questions

* L. Karakhan was Deputy People's Commissar for Foreign Affairs. The Declaration of July 25, 1919, was followed by a Soviet note to the Chinese government, in much the same terms, dated October 27, 1920.

provide convenient ammunition in the Sino-Soviet ideological argument? As a means of applying pressure, the Russian border is certainly of use to Peking; and it may be that the Chinese are now exploiting frontier policy in a manner analogous to the way in which the Russians used the frontiers of British India during the nineteenth century. It is hard to see how the Russians could now be induced to retreat from the boundaries which they inherited from the tsars without the application of armed force —in other words, without a Sino-Russian war.

Were it not for the Sino-Soviet political argument and all the imponderables which are in process of arising from it, there would be grounds for supposing that the Chinese attitude towards the Sino-Soviet border alignment could be compared, in some respects, with the Chinese view of the McMahon Line border between Tibet and India along the Assam Himalayas. It has been suggested that the Chinese objection to the McMahon Line lies, not in its geographical alignment (which is, in general, reasonable enough), but in its treaty basis, with implications of Tibetan sovereignty. The Chinese have made it clear that they dislike, even resent, the treaty basis for the Sino-Soviet border which, in their eyes, is a symbol of the period of the 'unequal' treaties and of imperialist aggression onto Chinese soil. At the same time, they seem to be prepared to admit that the actual course of the Sino-Soviet border is now an accomplished fact with which they must live. Thus, in early 1964, when Sino-Soviet relations were rapidly deteriorating, Chinese and Russian delegates none the less sat down to discuss the renegotiation of the Sino-Soviet border. The Chinese attitude on this occasion, so the *Peking Review* of May 8, 1964 put it, was as follows:

Although the old treaties relating to the Sino-Russian boundary are unequal treaties, the Chinese Government is nevertheless willing to respect them and take them as the basis for a reasonable settlement of the Sino-Soviet boundary question. Guided by proletarian internationalism and the principles governing relations between socialist countries, the Chinese Government will conduct friendly negotiations with the Soviet Government in the spirit of consultation on an equal footing and mutual understanding and mutual accommodation. If the Soviet side takes the same attitude as the Chinese Government, the settlement of the Sino-Soviet boundary question, we believe, ought not to be difficult, and the Sino-Soviet boundary will truly become one of lasting friendship.

In other words, provided the treaty basis is made 'equal', then the alignment can remain very much as it has been since tsarist times. Such an attitude on the part of the Chinese towards boundaries created in the colonial era should cause no surprise. It can, for example, be seen in the Sino-Burmese boundary agreement of 1960 and the Sino-Pakistani boundary agreement of 1963, in both of which the Chinese tacitly accepted the general outline of imperialist-imposed boundaries provided the treaty basis was seen to be post-imperialist: the product of the free choice of the Chinese People's Republic.

The long Sino-Soviet boundary is today as well-defined as any other stretch of the Chinese border. Only the extreme western end, in the Pamirs, has neither been delimited nor demarcated. The whole boundary is certainly far better defined than is the Sino-Indian border, and has been so for a long time. Yet the Sino-Soviet border has been changing rapidly in recent years, not in alignment, but in its basic nature. In the nineteenth century, it represented the divide between regions under tsarist authority and regions which, while under some degree of Chinese control, were not in fact inhabited by a Han Chinese majority. During the twentieth century, it has increasingly become a divide between regions of intense Chinese and Russian settlement. The Amur valley, for example, which a century ago was inhabited by scattered Tungus tribes, is now the meeting point of China at its most industrialised (in part, a product of the era of Japanese rule 1931–45) and of Russia in the form of great cities, like Khabarovsk, with hundreds of thousands of European inhabitants,* In Sinkiang, the Chinese population is increasing very rapidly indeed; in 1950, there were estimated to be only 300,000 Han Chinese in Sinkiang out of a total population of about 4 million; in 1962 there were, according to one source, 2 million Chinese out of a total of 7 million. While this Chinese growth was taking place, the Russians—as part of their 'virgin lands' programme of the middle 1950s—were putting a great deal of effort into an attempt to make Kazakhstan suitable for extensive agricultural settlement.

One consequence of economic development and population increase along the Sino-Soviet border has been to turn that border into the nearest Asian equivalent to the nation-state boundaries of Western Europe. The implications of this change are indeed far-reaching. From being a buffer zone separating two remote heartlands, the Sino-Soviet border is fast becoming (if it has not already done so) a region of direct confrontation of two highly developed nationalisms, but nationalisms competing for the loyalty of minorities: a process which carries with it an irredentist attitude towards similar minorities on the other side of the boundary line. The implications of this kind of situation are perhaps best illustrated in the modern frontier history of Germany.

* In the 1930s, the Soviet authorities also endeavoured to create a Jewish national home along the Amur, known as Birobidzhan or the Jewish Autonomous Oblast. The scheme was not a success, and the present Jewish population in the region is small.

Conclusions and Prospects

In the pre-colonial period, that region which we have called the Russian Zone was very much a marginal area on the frontier of the Iranian and Chinese spheres. The Southern Zone, which in our terminology embraces a tract from Iran to Vietnam, was divided between a number of civilisations and centres of political power. The Indian subcontinent, at the heart of the Southern Zone, possessed no real history of unity before the British conquest, the empires of Asoka and the Moghuls being exceptions rather than the rule. The Southern Zone was under constant pressure from the north-west; and in the north-east it lay on the steadily expanding south-western frontier of the Chinese world. In pre-colonial times, it was the Chinese Zone which possessed the most coherent history. The theme was the expansion of the Chinese state and the evolution of the land beyond the Great Wall into Chinese buffer tracts. There were periods when internal Chinese weakness enabled the nomads of Inner Asia to breach the defences of the Chinese Wall, but in each case a Chinese recovery followed. In the eighteenth century, at the height of the Manchu dynasty (itself with origins beyond the Wall), the Chinese were more powerful in Manchuria, Mongolia, Tibet and Eastern Turkestan than they had ever been before. In this period, Chinese influence was felt all along the divide between the Southern and Chinese zones, in the Himalayas and in the states of mainland South-east Asia.

In the colonial era, the balance between the three zones changed dramatically. The Russians spread across Siberia to the Pacific and then began to move southwards along the frontiers of China, Iran and the Indian subcontinent. This process began in the late sixteenth century, but reached its climax during the nineteenth century, when it was accompanied by British and French imperial expansion into the Southern Zone. By 1900, the entire Southern Zone was, in effect, under European control. Even those states—like Iran, Afghanistan, Nepal and Thailand—which were not actually subjected to outright European annexation, were still restricted to a considerable degree in their freedom of action by the application of imperial influence. Their boundaries and their foreign relations were determined by the three great European imperial powers on the Asian mainland: Russia, France and Britain. By the end of the first decade of the twentieth century, these three powers had become allied to each other in the context of European diplomacy.

Although disputes in Asia between the imperial powers did not disappear, in many ways the Southern Zone was able to behave as if it were a single power-block. As a result of discussions between the Russians, British and French—a process often beginning with active competition and ending with negotiations—both the internal and external boundaries and frontiers of the Southern Zone were devised. In the last analysis the stability of these boundaries and frontiers depended upon imperial co-operation. Imperial divisions often cut across traditional frontiers and, without the application of imperial pressure, these divisions would in many places have been challenged by indigenous bodies politic in the Southern Zone. It was Anglo-French diplomacy, for example, which both created and maintained the boundaries of Thailand. When Anglo-French influence was abruptly shattered here in 1941 by the

P

Japanese, one result was the modification of the boundaries of Thailand with Burma, Laos, Cambodia and Malaya—the Japanese giving to the Thais two Shan states, Laotian tracts along the Mekong, the Cambodian provinces of Siem Reap and Battembang, and the four Malay states of Perlis, Kedah, Kelantan and Trengganu which the British had acquired in 1909.

During the colonial era, China became weak, and the internal decay of the Manchu dynasty was accompanied by Russian, British and French pressure on its land frontiers. In the late nineteenth century, the three European powers were joined by the Japanese (who, for geographical reasons, have been rather ignored in this book).* During the first four and a half decades of the twentieth century, Japan attempted the total conquest of China and the permanent removal of Manchuria and Korea from the Chinese sphere. Japanese pressure was accompanied by Chinese civil war, which continued for almost five years after Japan's defeat in 1945. It was not until late 1949 that China once more emerged as a united state. From that point onwards, however, it rapidly acquired a power greater than that possessed by any dynasty. Manchuria, Inner Mongolia, Sinkiang and Tibet were brought under the complete control of the central government at Peking. Of the traditional Chinese frontier tracts in Central Asia, only Outer Mongolia remained without the Chinese fold.

* The Japanese soon began to influence boundary questions far removed from Manchuria and the China coast. In 1919, for example, the Chinese government approached the British with a view to continuing negotiations over the nature of the Sino-Tibetan border and its alignment: negotiations which China had broken off during the Simla Conference of 1913–14. No sooner had a real measure of Anglo-Chinese agreement on this question been reached than the Chinese again broke off negotiations. The reason, the British legation in Peking was convinced, was to be found in the application of Japanese pressure. It was clear by 1919, therefore, that it would be difficult to settle even the most westerly portions of the Chinese frontier without some reference to Japan.

In the 1950s, the Russians were in as complete control of their Asian zone as they had ever been. The divide between the Russian and Chinese zones now separated two monolithic powers with only one buffer section, Mongolia. Many observers have argued that, with the present deterioration of Sino-Soviet relations, major crises will now arise along the line of direct territorial contact of the two powers. So far this has not been the case. There have been tensions and disputes, but there has been nothing to compare with the confrontation along the Sino-Indian border. Indeed, in a curious way, the Sino-Russian border may be at least as stable today as it has ever been before. It is arguable that here, in contrast with the Southern Zone, the pattern of the imperial frontier system has been maintained. Neither Russia nor China can now expand territorially in this quarter without provoking armed conflict. Therefore, if we assume that a Sino-Russian war is not likely in the foreseeable future, then Sino-Russian border problems must, if they are to be solved at all, be solved by diplomatic means. There is in this, perhaps, an analogy with the situation between the British and the Russians when their mutual Asian frontier was being worked out. Crises there were, but they led to joint boundary commissions, not to war.

The Chinese communist regime may not like the treaty basis for its border with Russia. The Peking Treaty of 1860 and the St Petersburg Treaty of 1881, we have been left in no doubt, are regarded in Peking as 'unequal' treaties of the worst kind. They have, however, on the whole produced practical boundaries. From Mongolia to the Pacific Ocean, the Sino-Soviet border (except for short stretches at either end) follows a clear river line: that of the Argun, Amur and Ussuri. The Chinese may well feel that they have historical claims beyond this line, but it is hard to see on what criteria such claims would, in practice, be defined. It appears that, in the 1960s, there have been minor Sino-Russian boundary adjustments along the Amur, arising from the problem of the ownership of islands and

from shifts in river-courses. The implication is very much that
the Amur has been accepted *de facto* by the Chinese, however
reluctant they may be to acknowledge its treaty basis. The
western half of the Soviet-Sinkiang boundary, even though
some of its length has not been defined by treaty, also follows a
course dictated clearly enough by geography. The Aksu-Sarikol
watershed in the Pamirs and the crest of the western Tien Shan
range make admirable natural boundaries. The Chinese, while
they have denied any validity to the concept of natural boundaries (at least, as defined by Indian diplomatists), have, in
practice, appreciated their utility. The one 'unnatural' stretch
of Sino-Soviet border is that which divides eastern Sinkiang
from the Kazakh SSR. It is here that the Russians retained in
1881 a small tract of Sinkiang which they occupied in 1871, and
it is here that the boundary is a particularly unsatisfactory
ethnic divide. The Chinese could well press for a rectification of
the 1881 boundary along the Ili. The area involved is so small
that the Russians, in certain diplomatic circumstances, might
even agree to return it to China. The ethnic problem—that the
same people live on both sides of what is by no means an
impenetrable barrier—can only be solved by administrative
measures; and, no doubt, in normal circumstances this would
be done in due course.

For a third of its length, the Sino-Soviet frontier is shielded
by Mongolia. Some students of modern China have detected a
resolve in Peking that one day Mongolia shall be brought back
into the Chinese fold. It is true that Chinese leaders (in Taiwan
as well as in Peking) make statements, or permit publications,
which suggest that Mongolia is for ever engraved on their hearts.
In practice, however, the Chinese communist regime has fully
accepted the independence of Outer Mongolia; and in 1962 a
Sino-Mongolian boundary agreement was signed in which the
Chinese made concessions all along the long Mongolian border
with Sinkiang and Inner Mongolia. It would seem that both
Peking and Moscow appreciate the value of Mongolia as a buffer.

It would be reasonable to suppose, however, that the Chinese will seek at least to match Russian influence in Ulan Bator (Urga), the Mongol capital. In this respect, Mongolia may well become more like Afghanistan or Nepal: a buffer state where no single external influence is dominant.

A study of the Sino-Soviet border, *qua* boundary, rather suggests that in itself it poses but limited problems for future peace and stability. The real problem of the Sino-Soviet border lies in the fact that it *is* the Sino-Soviet border, that it divides two superpowers whose mutual relations have been deteriorating steadily for reasons not connected, in the main, with frontier issues. The uncertainties in boundary definition, the doubts concerning the validity or equitability of frontier treaties— these could well be used as ammunition in a major Sino-Soviet crisis with its real roots buried deep in ideological conflict or xenophobic instincts. Further, the border regions, with large non-Chinese minority populations on the Chinese side, might well become much disturbed in the event of a collapse of the authority of the Chinese central government over peripheral regions. Such a collapse—which would have seemed extremely improbable, to say the least, in 1963 or 1964—must now, against the background of the 'Great Cultural Revolution', be at least accorded the status of a theoretical possibility.

While it would seem that, along the junction of the Chinese and Russian zones, major frontier crises are more likely to be the result of diplomatic crises than the other way about, along the frontiers of the Southern Zone there remains a very real possibility that, in post-colonial Asia, boundary problems will still, in their own right, continue to have important diplomatic consequences. While in each of the other two zones the diplomatic initiative is held by a single government, so that interzonal boundary problems can be dealt with by bipartite diplomacy, in the Southern Zone the initiative is held by a large number of states, many of them at daggers-drawn with their neighbours. It is hard to imagine at this time, for example, a joint Indo-Pakistani frontier policy *vis-à-vis* China—at least, not until the Kashmir problem is solved. The diplomatic control exercised by the French and the British has not been replaced by that of any one independent Asian power. There are, in fact, a number of power-vacua in the Southern Zone today, and the old imperial frontier system cannot withstand the resultant external pressures. Where, before the period 1947–54, the French and the British looked after the entire southern Chinese frontier from the Pamirs to the Gulf of Tonkin, that task has now been delegated to at least six independent states with virtually no common interests.

Were the Southern Zone left to its own devices, a state of equilibrium between its component states and the Chinese People's Republic would be reached quickly enough. Sinophobes and those who believe in an 'aggressive' China would no doubt be convinced that, in these circumstances, the Chinese would 'take over' the entire Southern Zone, with the possible exception of Iran—which would, doubtless, be 'taken over' by the Soviet Union. There are others, among whom the author of this book must be numbered, who do not think that China has any strong territorial ambitions in a colonial sense outside its established traditional sphere. Even so, however, faced with a power-vacuum in the Southern Zone, the Chinese could not fail to establish within it a series of 'protectorates', as that term is understood in the context of frontier policy. Burma, perhaps, provides us with a model of such a 'protectorate'. Peking's foreign policy is designed to prevent any threats, military or political, from being directed, or seeming to be directed, against China from Burmese soil. The Chinese, satisfied by the shape of Burmese foreign policy, make no attempt to intervene in Burmese internal affairs.

China's abstention from meddling in the internal affairs of neighbouring states, however, would depend upon two criteria being satisfied. First: the central government of the given state would have to be able to maintain the control over its population. Civil war just across the Chinese frontier would be a standing temptation for Chinese interference, just as trans-frontier disturbances induced British and Russian intervention in various Asian regions in the nineteenth century. Chinese intervention, moreover, would inevitably result in the expansion of Chinese ideology. Second: China would not allow a regime actively hostile to the prevailing Chinese ideology the unopposed government of any state along its frontiers. A violently anti-communist regime adjacent to China could only be seen in Peking, and perhaps rightly so, as a threat to Chinese frontier security. The trend of an unopposed Chinese domination of the states along its frontier in the Southern Zone, therefore, would be towards the creation or encouragement of regimes avoiding political commitments to the West and socialist in outlook, if not actually communist. There could be no exceptions as far as political alignment was concerned, though it is not impossible to imagine non-marxist states co-existing happily enough with China if they were also suitably non-aligned.

This trend the United States of America has now resolved to oppose. In so doing, at least in the field of frontier policy, America has assumed the mantle of the British and the French, the former colonial masters of the Southern Zone. The wisdom of this resolve it is not our task to question here; there can be no doubt that, if only tacitly, the decision has been made. We must consider its implication for the future history of boundaries and frontiers on the Asian mainland.

★

The Americans do not have the freedom of action in the Southern Zone which the British and French enjoyed. The territorial limits of the independent states of the Southern Zone, as we have seen, were largely determined, directly or indirectly, by the needs of imperial frontier policy. These states, and their boundaries and frontiers, the Americans have, as it were, inherited; at present there is little they can do to change them. The modern frontier problem of Asia, at least in American eyes, is the containment of the two great communist powers, Russia and China. As far as Russia is concerned, the old imperial frontier system has proved quite easy to transfer to American hands. American influence in Iran and Afghanistan does today more or less what the British hoped the Anglo-Russian Convention of 1907 would do. Along the edges of the Chinese world, however, the old imperial frontier system has not been so satisfactory.

Neither the British nor the French in the great days of imperial frontier construction were particularly concerned about the Chinese danger. The British Indian frontier with Tibet was really part of the defences against Russia; it was not intended to withstand the pressure of a powerful and united Chinese state, for such did not exist in the British period. The whole of Chinese Central Asia was, in the eyes of British imperial strategists, an Anglo-Russian buffer. The Chinese could be a nuisance, but they were not a major threat. Thus, it was possible to leave undefined long stretches of the British border with Sinkiang and Tibet. The British knew that, in the last resort, they could deal with border problems here of Chinese origin by means of the application of diplomatic pressure in Peking.

On occasions, of course, there was trouble along the Indian northern and north-eastern frontiers of British India which could not be ignored. The Tibetan occupation of a portion of Sikkim in 1886, for example, produced a train of events which culminated in the delimitation of the Sikkim-Tibet boundary by Anglo-Chinese treaty in 1890. The Chinese penetration into the northern fringes of the Assam Himalayas in the period 1910–12 is another example, and it produced the McMahon Line of 1914. It should be noted, however, that neither the Sikkim-Tibet boundary of 1890 nor the McMahon Line of 1914 was, in fact, created in the face of active Chinese opposition on the ground. The 1890 boundary between Sikkim and Tibet was designed to exclude the Tibetans, whom the Chinese had proved themselves unable to control. The McMahon Line, though in many ways an anti-Chinese device, came into being at a moment when China was no longer in physical control of territory adjacent to it. The Chinese actions of 1910–12 may have provoked the British into thinking about a northward advance of their Outer Line boundary in Assam, but they were able to bring this advance about only after 1912, when the Chinese Revolution had brought about a collapse in China's position in Tibet. Only along the Burma-Yunnan frontier did the British meet consistent Chinese resistance; and here, because the boundary was created through joint Anglo-Chinese action on the ground—even though in places sanctified by no treaty and in conflict with Chinese theoretical claims—the British line has, with very minor modification, proved adequate to meet the needs of Sino-Burmese relations in the age of Asian independence.

In Indochina, the French also faced a China which could be controlled better by diplomatic pressure than by the mounting of transfrontier campaigns. The French after 1886 had no real fear of a Chinese invasion of Tonkin or Laos. The result was a border between French Indochina and China defined clearly enough, but it was a border which the French did not see as a kind of Maginot Line against Chinese attack. Indeed, many French colonial strategists anticipated that beyond it would lie a growing French sphere of influence in Yunnan. The major French concern during their great period of colonial acquisition in mainland South-east Asia was their relations with the British, the other great power in the region. The primary aim of France's frontier policy was in the devising of a stable Anglo-French demarcation.

In building their frontier systems, the British and French possessed control over the internal affairs of the regions whose limits they were setting. They could add a bit here and take away a bit there without having to worry too much about Asian opinion. They did not mind being called imperialists. The Americans, at present, do not possess this control. They are not an imperial power on the Asian mainland; they are there as the protectors of indigenous Asian states, and are committed to the boundaries of those states as they were brought about by the British and the French. This fact has already added greatly to the American difficulties in Vietnam, confronting the United States with one of the fundamental problems of frontier policy.

The Americans are defending South Vietnam and struggling to keep in being there a regime which meets their political and strategic requirements. In other words, as the old imperialists would have put it, they are trying to keep South Vietnam in their sphere of influence. The immediate threat to South Vietnam, they are convinced, comes from North Vietnam. Hanoi supports the Viet Cong; in fighting the Viet Cong in South Vietnam, the United States has felt itself obliged to attack North Vietnam from the air. In other words, in order to prevent the North Vietnamese from penetrating the line of demarcation of the 17th Parallel, the Americans have had to cross that Parallel. This is a situation familiar to the old imperialists, who would have seen it leading inevitably, and with much protestation on their part that they had no such intentions, to an annexation of North Vietnam. Indeed, by this kind of process, Tonkin became French in the 1880s. In the defence of South Vietnam, however, it is not only the 17th Parallel that must be watched. The Viet Cong certainly receive supplies by way of Laos, and they may do so through Cambodia as well. Thus, the Americans must face the possibility that they will have to extend their operations across the Cambodia–South Vietnam and Laos–South Vietnam boundaries as well as the 17th Parallel between North and South Vietnam. The defence of South Vietnam involves, therefore, the whole of what used to be French Indochina. The problem of the Laos–South Vietnam border, moreover, is closely related to the problem of the security of north-east Thailand and the west bank of the Mekong; and here is a further extension of the outer glacis of South Vietnamese frontiers.

As yet, the Americans have been inclined to adopt for the protection of the glacis a modern version of the old gunboat diplomacy. Punitive bombardment, it is hoped, will do the job without the application of control on the ground. States under strong central governments, like North Vietnam, may well in the end decide that they have seen enough gunboats of the air and come to a boundary agreement which they are capable of enforcing on their side. It is hard to see how such boundary agreements could be imposed upon Laos and Cambodia, which are at present under regimes without the power adequately to police their frontier tracts. Laos and Cambodia call for something more than air power.

American civil and military leaders talk of Vietnam in ideological terms. They are helping the South Vietnamese to maintain their freedom in the face of a communist aggression that is encouraged, aided and abetted by Hanoi; and behind Hanoi lies Peking (not to mention Moscow). Hanoi and Peking also use the language of ideology. They are helping to liberate the people of South Vietnam from the yoke of American imperialism. To some extent, no doubt, both sides really see the issue in these terms. It cannot have escaped the notice of both sides, however, that they are also involved in a frontier struggle along the classic pattern of the old empires. What the American 'domino theory' really means is that, unless a line can be maintained in the South-east Asian mainland, the whole area will fall under Chinese influence. The struggle is about where exactly that line will be drawn. Can it be made to coincide with the lines which emerged as a result of French and British colonial expansion?

The answer, it seems most probable, is no. When China was weak, the imperial powers could afford to be in direct territorial contact with Chinese territory. Today, as the Korean war showed clearly enough, such contact is fraught with danger; and American strategy appears to have come to this conclusion. North Vietnam, like North Korea, must remain a buffer between the Chinese and American spheres. Can South Vietnam, assuming American success in the present conflict, remain an adequate bastion of American influence without a modification of colonial boundaries? The major problem lies in Laos, where there already exists an unofficial division into American and buffer tracts. The present partition of Laos, however, does not satisfy the strategic requirements of South Vietnam; it never will until, even if in a most indirect way, the 17th Parallel is extended westwards to the Mekong. Laos, of course, also involves the security of the second American bastion on the South-east Asian mainland: Thailand. Some kind of frontier here must be established along the line of hills to the east of the Mekong, if the course of the Mekong itself is not to be accepted as the boundary.

In the creation of a new frontier in mainland South-east Asia, the Thais have a key role. Unless the Americans are prepared to resort to physical conquest, they must purchase the continued loyalty of the Thais. In the long run, the price could well involve boundary changes in Thailand's favour. An advance into Cambodia is one possibility; the transfer to Thailand of Laotian territory on the west bank of the Mekong is another. The net result of such modifications in the Anglo-French frontier system would be an American enclave on the Asian mainland: a giant version of South Korea, separated from China by North Vietnam, northern Laos and Burma. This enclave would serve as the forward line in the defence of Malaysia, the Philippines and Indonesia, behind which lies Australasia. To the theorists of nineteenth- and early twentieth-century frontier policy, such a settlement would not appear unreasonable.

The right flank of this forward line would be the point where the 17th Parallel meets the sea. Its stability would depend upon the ability of the United States to create a stable South Vietnam. The left flank is Burma. At present, Burma meets the requirements of both Chinese and American frontier policy, and it could continue to do so even if the regime relaxed a little its exclusion of Western influences. Burma, however, would pose grave problems if the central government in Rangoon found itself unable to retain its present degree of control over the outlying districts. A major Burmese civil war, particularly one with ideological as well as ethnic overtones, would invite the intervention, at least covertly, of the Americans from their position in Thailand. The final outcome could well be a redefining of Burmese boundaries. It would be difficult to imagine, for example, the United States' acquiescing in the establishment of active Chinese influence in Tenasserim: that strip of Burmese coast leading to the overseas Chinese populations of the Kra Isthmus and the Malay peninsula.

Burma, at the present moment, keeps the two great frontier problems of the Southern Zone apart. On the east is Vietnam and the mainland South-east Asian crisis; on the west is the unresolved Sino-Indian confrontation along the Himalayas. India is too big, and potentially too powerful, to become a satisfactory buffer zone along the Chinese frontier. The direct contact of Chinese and Indian administered territory along frontier tracts with undefined boundaries cannot fail to go on producing tension. Yet India is unable, with its own resources, to meet China on equal terms and is not prepared to face the political and diplomatic consequences of negotiating the Sino-Indian boundary from a position of weakness. Thus, India has tended to drift—albeit reluctantly—into the American sphere. The result would have been more satisfactory from the Indian point of view had it not been for the existence of Pakistan and the great frontier dispute over Kashmir. The state of Jammu and Kashmir, situated at the trijunction of India, Pakistan and China, has been the Achilles-heel in the late Pandit Nehru's policy of non-alignment. From the outset, India had been aligned against Pakistan, hence its enemies have tended to be aligned with Pakistan. The result of the Sino-Indian conflict, therefore, has been a Sino-Pakistani relationship which, even in its present embryonic form, has brought a significant measure of Chinese influence through the mountain frontier of the sub-continent to the shores of the Indian Ocean.

There are a number of possibilities inherent in the frontier situation of the Indian subcontinent, but there is not the space here to speculate about them. The problems created by the modern irrelevance of British frontier policy in the Himalayas and the Karakoram, when complicated by the Kashmir dispute —to a considerable degree an uncompleted piece of business arising from the process of partition of the British Indian empire in 1947—can be resolved only through the evolution of a completely new kind of frontier policy. Such a policy would involve the defining of some fresh boundaries. Something would have to be done about Kashmir: possibly a partition on com-munal lines. A kind of buffer might have to be created out of the tribal hills of Assam.

We have some grounds for supposing that the boundaries of the Southern Zone in Asia are not for ever fixed, like the laws of the Medes and the Persians. Perhaps we are at this time in a transitional period between the frontier system of the old European empires and the new frontier system of the American and Chinese spheres of influence on the Asian mainland. The first stage of this process, the transfer of power from European to Asian rule, has now been completed. The next stage, the determination of the territorial limits of that rule and the nature of American and Chinese influence over it, may perhaps be just beginning. The Second World War has been followed by drama-tic changes in the pattern of power in Asia: changes comparable with those which occurred in Europe and the Near East after the First World War. Just as the collapse of the Austro-Hungarian and Ottoman empires introduced a period of major boundary readjustment, so may it be that the end of the British and French empires in the East, once its consequences have had full time to take effect, will usher in a new age of frontier-building. If so, then the study of frontier policy, its history and its nature, is a subject of more than academic interest.

Bibliography

The books whose titles are listed below are some of the more useful works in any attempt to study the frontier history of the Asian continent. No attempt has been made here to compile anything approaching a comprehensive bibliography. Articles in periodicals have been omitted as well as works in languages other than English, French and German.

GENERAL

Adami, V., *National Frontiers in Relation to International Law*, trans. by T. T. Behrens, Humphrey Milford, London 1927

Ancel, J., *Les Frontières*, Paris 1938

Boggs, S. W., *International Boundaries: A Study of Boundary Functions and Problems*, Columbia University Press, New York 1940; Oxford University Press, London 1940

Cornish, V., *Borderlands of Language in Europe and their relation to the historic frontiers of Christendom*, Sifton, Praed, London 1936

Cressey, G. B., *Asia's Lands and Peoples*, 3rd edn, McGraw-Hill, New York 1963

Curzon, Lord, *Frontiers* (Romanes Lecture), Oxford University Press, Oxford 1907

East, W. G., *The Geography Behind History*, London 1965

———— and Spate, O. H. K., *The Changing Map of Asia*, Methuen, London 1950; E. P. Dutton, New York 1951

Fawcett, C. B., *Frontiers: A Study in Political Geography*, Oxford University Press, Oxford 1918

Fieldhouse, D. K., *The Colonial Empires*, Dell, New York 1966; Weidenfeld and Nicolson, London 1966

Goblet, Y. M., *Political Geography and the World Map*, Philip, London 1955; Praeger, New York 1955

Grousset, R., *L'Empire des Steppes*, Paris 1948

Haushofer, K., *Grenzen*, Berlin 1927

Hill, N. L., *Claims to Territory in International Law and Relations*, Oxford University Press, London and New York 1945

Holdich, Sir T. H., *Political Frontiers and Boundary Making*, Macmillan, London 1916

Jones, S. B., *Boundary-Making: A Handbook for Statesmen*, Columbia University Press, New York 1945

Lapradelle, P. de, *La Frontière*, Paris 1929

Lehault, P., *La France et l'Angleterre en Asie*, Paris 1892

Mackinder, Sir H., *Democratic Ideals and Reality*, Constable, London 1919

Prescott, J. R. V., *The Geography of Frontiers and Boundaries*, Hutchinson, London 1965; Hillary House, New York 1965

Rawlinson, Sir H., *England and Russia in the East*, London 1875

Stahl, K. M., *British and Soviet Colonial Systems*, Faber, London 1951; Praeger, New York 1951

Wint, G., *The British in Asia*, Faber, London 1947

IRAN, AFGHANISTAN, PAKISTAN AND INDIA

Alder, G. J., *British India's Northern Frontier 1865–95: A Study in Imperial Policy*, Longmans, London 1963

Avery, P., *Modern Iran*, Benn, London 1965; Praeger, New York 1965

Bains, J. S., *India's International Disputes: A Legal Study*, Asia Publishing House, London 1962, New York 1963

Barton, Sir W., *India's North-West Frontier*, Murray, London 1939

Birdwood, Lord, *Two Nations and Kashmir*, Hale, London 1956

Brecher, M., *The Struggle for Kashmir*, Oxford University Press, New York and London 1953

Callard, K., *Pakistan: A Political Study*, Macmillan, New York 1957; Allen and Unwin, London 1957

Caroe, Sir O., *The Pathans, 550 BC–AD 1957*, 2nd edn, Macmillan, London 1962; St Martin's Press, New York 1962

Curzon, G. N., *Persia and the Anglo-Persian Question*, London 1892

Davies, C. C., *The Problem of the Northwest Frontier, 1890–1908*, Cambridge University Press, Cambridge 1932

Fraser-Tytler, Sir W. K. (revised edn, Sir M. C. Gillett), *Afghanistan: A Study of Political Developments in Central and Southern Asia*, Oxford University Press, London and New York 1967

Greaves, R. L., *Persia and the Defence of India, 1884–1892*, Athlone Press, London 1959; Essential Books, New York 1959

Gupta, A., *Politics in Nepal*, Bombay 1964

Gupta, S., *Kashmir: A Study in India-Pakistan Relations*, Asia Publishing House, New York 1966, London 1967

Holdich, Sir T. H., *The Indian Borderland 1880–1900*, 2nd edn, Methuen, London 1909

———— *The Gates of India*, 2nd edn, Methuen, London 1914

Jain, G., *India meets China in Nepal*, Bombay 1959

Karan, P. P., and Jenkins, W. M., *The Himalayan Kingdoms: Bhutan, Sikkim and Nepal*, Van Nostrand, Princeton, N.J. 1963

Korbel, J., *Danger in Kashmir*, Princeton University Press, Princeton, N.J. 1954

Lamb, A., *The China-India Border: The Origins of the Disputed Boundaries*, Oxford University Press, London and New York 1964

———— *The McMahon Line: A Study in the Relations Between India, China and Tibet, 1904 to 1914*, 2 Vols, Routledge and Kegan Paul, London 1966; University of Toronto Press, Toronto 1966

———— *Crisis in Kashmir 1947–1966*, Routledge and Kegan Paul, London 1966; published in the United States as *The Kashmir Problem: A Historical Survey*, Praeger, New York 1967

Macgregor, Sir C., *The Defence of India*, Simla 1884

Menon, V. P., *The Story of the Integration of the Indian States*, Longmans, London 1956; Macmillan, New York 1956

———— *The Transfer of Power in India*, Longmans, London and Calcutta 1957; Princeton University Press, Princeton, N.J. 1959

Patterson, G. N., *Peking versus Delhi*, Faber, London 1963; Praeger, New York 1964

Richardson, H. E., *Tibet and its History*, Oxford University Press, London and New York 1960

Smith, V. A. (ed. T. G. P. Spear), *The Oxford History of India*, 3rd edn, Oxford University Press, London and New York 1958

Spate, O. H. K., *India and Pakistan*, Methuen, London 1957

Stephens, I., *Pakistan*, rev. edn, Benn, London 1966; Praeger, New York 1967

Sykes, Sir P., *A History of Afghanistan*, 2 vols, Macmillan, London 1940, New York 1941

———— *A History of Persia*, 3rd edn, 2 vols, Macmillan, London 1930

Symonds, R., *The Making of Pakistan*, Faber, London 1950; Transatlantic Arts, Hollywood, Fla. 1950

Tinker, H., *South Asia: A Short History*, Pall Mall, London 1966; Praeger, New York 1966

Tuker, Sir F., *Gorkha: The Story of the Gurkhas of Nepal*, Constable, London 1957

Wilber, D. N., *Pakistan*, Yale University Press, New Haven, Conn. 1964

Wilcox, W. A., *Pakistan: The Consolidation of a Nation*, Columbia University Press, New York 1963

―――― *India, Pakistan and the Rise of China*, Walker, New York 1964

Younghusband, G. J., *Indian Frontier Warfare*, London 1898

SOUTH-EAST ASIA

Abadie, M., *Les Races du Haut-Tonkin*, Paris 1924

Buchanan, K., *The Southeast Asian World*, George Bell, London 1967; Taplinger, New York 1967

Buttinger, J., *The Smaller Dragon. A Political History of Vietnam*, Praeger, New York 1958, and London 1966

Chesneaux, J., *Contribution à l'Histoire de la Nation Vietnamienne*, Paris 1955

Cady, J. F., *The Roots of French Imperialism in Eastern Asia*, Cornell University Press, Ithaca, New York 1954

Christian, J. L., *Modern Burma: A Survey of Political and Economic Developments*, University of California Press, Berkeley, Calif. 1942

Coedès, G., *The Making of South East Asia*, Routledge and Kegan Paul, London 1966; University of California Press, Berkeley, Calif. 1966

Deydier, H., *Introduction à la Connaissance du Laos*, Paris 1952

Dobby, E. H. C., *Southeast Asia*, University of London Press, London 1950

Embree, J. P., and Dotson, L. O., *A Bibliography of the Peoples and Cultures of Mainland South-East Asia*, Yale University Press, New Haven, Conn. 1950

Fisher, C. A., *South-east Asia*, Methuen, London 1964; E. P. Dutton, New York 1964

Hall, D. G. E., *A History of South-East Asia*, Macmillan, London 1955; St Martin's Press, New York 1955

Harvey, G. E., *History of Burma*, Longmans, London 1925

―――― *British Rule in Burma, 1824–1942*, Faber, London 1946

Hunter, G., *South-East Asia: Race, Culture and Nation*, Oxford University Press, London and New York 1966

Kunstadter, P. (ed.), *South East Asia: Tribes, Minorities and Nations*, 2 vols., Princeton University Press, Princeton, N.J. 1967

Lancaster, D., *The Emancipation of French Indochina*, Oxford University Press, London and New York 1961

Le Thanh Khoi, *Le Vietnam, histoire et civilisation*, Paris 1955

LeBar, F. M., and Suddard, A., ed. *Laos: Its People, Its Society, Its Culture*, Hraf Press, New Haven, Conn. 1963

Leifer, M., *Cambodia: The Search for Security*, Praeger, New York 1967; Pall Mall, London 1968

Masson, A., *Histoire du Vietnam*, Paris 1960

Maybon, C. B., *Histoire Moderne du Pays d'Annam, 1592–1829*, Paris 1920

Nguyen Van Huyen, *La Civilisation Annamite*, Hanoi 1943

Pavie, A., *A la conquête des coeurs*, Paris 1921

Pendleton, R. L., *Thailand*, Duell, Sloane and Pearce, New York 1962

Reinach, L. de, *Le Laos*, 2 vols, Paris 1911

Robequain, C., *L'Indochine Francaise*, Paris 1935

Roberts, S. H., *History of French Colonial Policy, 1870–1925*, 2 vols, P. S. King, London 1929

Rose, S. (ed.), *Politics in Southern Asia*, Macmillan, London 1963; St Martin's Press, New York 1963

Scott, J. G., *France and Tongking*, London 1885

Scott, Sir J. G., *Burma, from the earliest times to the present day*, T. Fisher Unwin, London 1924

Shakespear, Col. L. W., *History of Upper Assam, Upper Burmah and North-Eastern Frontier*, Macmillan, London 1914

Smith, R. M., *Cambodia's Foreign Policy*, Cornell University Press, Ithaca, New York 1965

Steinberg, D. J. (revised edn, H. J. Vreeland), *Cambodia*, Yale University Press, New Haven, Conn. 1959

Tinker, H., *The Union of Burma: A Study of the First Years of Independence*, 3rd edn, London 1961

Trager, F. N., *Burma: From Kingdom to Republic*, Praeger, New York 1966; Pall Mall, London 1966

Wood, W. A. R., *History of Siam*, T. Fisher Unwin, London 1926

Woodman, D., *The Making of Burma*, Cresset Press, London 1962

Young, G., *The Hill Tribes of Northern Thailand*, Bangkok 1962

RUSSIA AND CHINA

Ambekar, G. V., and Divekar, V. D., *Documents on China's Relations with South and South-East Asia 1949–1962*, Bombay 1964

Baddeley, J. F., *Russia, Mongolia, China*, 2 vols, Macmillan, London 1919

Barthold, V. V., *La Découverte de l'Asie*, Paris 1947

Beasley, W. G., *The Modern History of Japan*, Weidenfeld and Nicolson, London 1963; Praeger, New York 1963

Buchan, A. (ed.), *China and the Peace of Asia*, Chatto and Windus, London 1965; Praeger, New York 1965

Cahen, G., *Histoire des Relations de la Russie avec la Chine, 1689–1730*, Paris 1912

Caroe, Sir O., *Soviet Empire: the Turks of Central Asia and Stalinism*, Macmillan, London 1953

Carruthers, D., *Unknown Mongolia*, 2 vols, Hutchinson, London 1913

Cheng Tien-fong, *A History of Sino-Soviet Relations*, Public Affairs Press, Washington 1957

Cordier, H., *Histoire des Relations de La Chine avec les Puissances Occidentales 1860–1900*, 3 vols, Paris 1901–2

—————— *Histoire Générale de la Chine et de ses relations avec les pays étrangers depuis les temps les plus anciens jusqu'à la chute de la dynastie mandchoue*, 4 vols, Paris 1920–21

Cressey, G. B., *Land of 500 Million: A Geography of China*, McGraw-Hill, New York 1955, London 1956

Curzon, G. N., *Russia in Central Asia and the Anglo-Russian Question*, London 1889

Dallin, D. J., *Soviet Russia and the Far East*, Yale University Press, New Haven, Conn. 1948

—————— *The Rise of Russia in Asia*, Yale University Press, New Haven, Conn. 1949

Doolin, D. J., *Territorial Claims in the Sino-Soviet Conflict*, Stanford University Press, Stanford, Calif. 1965

Fairbank, J. K., Reischauer, E. O., and Craig, A. M., *East Asia: The Modern Transformation*, Houghton Mifflin, Boston 1965; Allen and Unwin, London 1965

Fitzgerald, C. P., *The Chinese View of their Place in the World*, Oxford University Press, London and New York 1964

Friters, G. M., *Outer Mongolia and its International Position*, John Hopkins Press, Baltimore 1949; Oxford University Press, London 1950

Hambly, G. (ed.), *Zentralasien* (Fischer Weltgeschichte Vol. 16), Frankfort-on-Main 1966

Harrison, J. A., *Japan's Northern Frontier*, University of Florida Press, Gainesville, Fla. 1953

Hertslet, Sir E., *Treaties, &c., between Great Britain and China; and between China and Foreign Powers; and Orders in Council, Rules, Regulations, Acts of Parliament, Decrees, and Notifications affecting British interests in China: in force on the 1st January, 1896*. Vol 1, London 1896

Hsü, I. C. Y., *The Ili Crisis: A Study of Sino-Russian Diplomacy, 1878–1881*, Oxford University Press, London and New York 1965

Jackson, W. A. D., *Russo-Chinese Borderlands*, Van Nostrand, Princeton, N.J. 1962

Kolarz, W., *Russia and Her Colonies*, Philip, London 1952; Praeger, New York 1952

—— *The Peoples of the Soviet Far East*, Philip, London 1954; Praeger, New York 1954

Lattimore, O., *The Mongols of Manchuria*, John Day, New York 1934; Allen and Unwin, London 1935

—— *Inner Asian Frontiers of China*, Capitol Publishers, New York 1951

—— *Pivot of Asia*, Little, Brown, Boston 1950, London 1952

Lensen, G. A., *The Russian Push Towards Japan: Russo-Japanese Relations 1697–1875*, University of Princeton Press, Princeton, N.J. 1959

Lévine, J., *La Mongolie: historique, géographique, politique*, Paris 1937

Li, T.-T., *The Historical Status of Tibet*, Kings Crown Press, New York 1956

Lobanov-Rostovsky, Prince, *Russia and Asia*, Macmillan, London and New York 1933

Morse, H. B., *The International Relations of the Chinese Empire*, 3 vols, Longmans, London 1910–18

Murphy, G. G. S., *Soviet Mongolia. A Study of the Oldest Political Satellite*, University of California Press, Berkeley, Calif. 1966

Pierce, R. A., *Russian Central Asia, 1867–1917*, University of California Press, Berkeley, Calif. 1960

Rupen, R. A., *Mongols of the Twentieth Century*, 2 vols, Mouton, The Hague 1964

Schuyler, E., *Turkistan: Notes of a Journey in Russian Turkistan, Khokand, Bukhara and Kuldja*, 2 vols, 1876; new edn (ed. Geoffrey E. Wheeler), Routledge and Kegan Paul, London 1966; Praeger, New York 1966

Sebes, J., *The Jesuits and the Sino-Russian Treaty of Nerchinsk*, Rome 1961

Shabad, T., *China's Changing Map*, Praeger, New York 1956; Methuen, London 1956

Tang, P. S. H., *Russian and Soviet Policy in Manchuria and Outer Mongolia, 1911–1931*, Duke University Press, Durham, N.C. 1959

Treaties and Agreements with and concerning China, 1894–1919, 2 vols, Carnegie Endowment for International Peace, Washington 1921

Watson, F., *The Frontiers of China: A Historical Guide*, Chatto and Windus, London 1966; Praeger, New York 1966

Wheeler, G., *The Modern History of Soviet Central Asia*, Weidenfeld and Nicolson, London 1964; Praeger, New York 1965

—— *The Peoples of Soviet Central Asia*, Bodley Head, London 1966; Dufour, Chester Springs, Pa. 1966

Whiting, A. S., and Sheng Shih-ts'ai, *Sinkiang: Pawn or Pivot?*, New York 1954

Wiens, H. J., *China's March Toward the Tropics*, Shoe String Press, Hamden, Conn. 1954

Wu, A. K., *China and the Soviet Union*, John Day, New York 1950

Yakhontoff, V. A., *Russia and the Soviet Union in the Far East*, Allen and Unwin, London 1932

Index